The Comprehension
Toolkit
Language and Lessons for Active Literacy

Stephanie Harvey & Anne Goudvis

The Source Book of Short Text

*first*hand
An imprint of Heinemann
361 Hanover Street
Portsmouth, NH 03801-3912
firsthand.heinemann.com
Offices and agents throughout the world

ISBN 0-325-00583-4

Printed in the United States of America on acid-free paper

15 14 13 12   ML   7 8 9 10

Lesson Texts

Short Text

For the list of *Short Text Titles,* see page 91.

The Source Book
OF SHORT TEXT

Introduction

We've gathered all the exemplary text that accompanies or extends each lesson into one handy reproducible book for you. In the *Source Book,* you'll find two kinds of text:

Lesson Text

Each of the twenty-six lessons is built around an engaging exemplary text that we've tested in classrooms across the country and can guarantee students find engaging. When you introduce kids to the *Toolkit* strategies, it's important that you use text that naturally appeals to kids and will almost certainly captivate them. We recommend that you make overheads of this text. As you introduce the lessons, you'll find it helpful to have the text up on a screen so your kids can easily follow along with you. Note that not all of the lesson text is included in the *Source Book*; for example, some of the lessons are built on picture books which you may find in your classroom or school library; if not, consider purchasing the optional *Trade Book Pack.*

The Lesson Texts include text written and designed especially for kids, including kids magazine articles, an Internet article, two poems, two excerpts from a nonfiction series and a U.S. History chapter. "Stealing Beauty," an article from TIME Magazine, is the one exception, as it is written with adults in mind. We chose "Stealing Beauty" to demonstrate how we use *Toolkit* strategies in our own reading process.

Nonfiction Short Text

We typically use short nonfiction text to introduce kids to strategic reading because it's inherently interesting and engaging even to the most reluctant readers. Additionally, short text presents a complete set of thoughts and ideas and doesn't take long to read. The teachers with whom we work immediately recognize the value of our short nonfiction text and they want to know where they can get their hands on some, too. Truth is we're always on the lookout for engaging short text we can share with kids; indeed, we've been known to tear fun, lively essays from airplane magazines. However, you don't have to fly to get good short text. We make it easier for you and supply you with *Nonfiction Short Text*, a text pack of 42 short pieces specially written for the *Toolkit* about a range of topics we chose, knowing they would appeal to kids—everything from Lance Armstrong to the greenhouse effect. Note we've organized the *Short Text* thematically and by reading challenge. Nearly every thematic grouping includes stories that are easy to read and others that offer a greater challenge. Who knows? As you enjoy these with your students, perhaps they'll be inspired to write their own "Shorts."

Ruthless art thieves are rapidly stripping Asia's cultural sites of precious artifacts and selling them to smugglers and dealers who hawk them in the West. A TIME Special Report. By Hannah Beech

Stealing Beauty

THE CITIZENS OF XIAOLI VILLAGE MOVE LAZILY, with a languor born of chronic underemployment. They are farmers by tradition, but exorbitant taxes have leached any profitability out of their profession. So on most hot days, the local peasants sit on concrete stoops, pant legs hiked up to their thighs, fanning themselves with the latest propaganda broadsheet from Beijing and waiting for dusk to fall. For it is only at night that Xiaoli comes alive.

Underneath this sad little village in Henan province is the rich legacy of five millenniums of Chinese history. The nearby city of Luoyang was the capital of at least nine dynasties, and the fields of today's peasants are littered with imperial tombs. Many still hold impossibly valuable works of art buried centuries ago. Breaking into these tombs and stealing the national treasures they hold are illegal, of course. But the lure is too great for many, especially because one major haul, sold to a smuggler, can equal a year's farming income. "For kids here, tomb raiding is just like going to the bar," says Little Su, a Xiaoli doctor who put himself through medical school with the spoils of treasure hunts beneath the fields around his home. "If you're bored one night, someone will say, 'Hey, let's go find a tomb.'" The rewards of these amateur and often dangerous nocturnal expeditions are evident in Little Su's wardrobe—he has long since traded in baggy peasant garb for snazzy Playboy shirts and gleaming loafers—and in the incongruous mishmash of mud-brick shacks and shiny white-tiled

houses with satellite dishes lining the streets of Xiaoli. "You can tell who raided the best tombs just by looking at their houses," says Little Su. The richest citizens even have big-screen TVs and video-game machines. Little Su's favorite game? *Tomb Raider*.

Archaeologists like to joke that the pillaging of temples and other ancient sites is the world's second oldest profession. But what used to be a trickle of plundered treasures has become a flood in recent years. Villagers like Little Su, who see nothing wrong in converting an untapped resource into a few modern consumer appliances, are merely the first link in a global antiquities-smuggling chain that the U.N. says rivals the drug and arms trades in scope and scale. Says Kathryn Tubb, conservator of the Institute of Archaeology at University College of London: "It's commonly accepted by those of us who work in the field that 80% to 90% of the material on the market is illicit."

The trade in Asian relics—whether obtained legally or looted—is booming, driven by demand from wealthy Western and Eastern collectors seeking to decorate their SoHo lofts and Shanghai penthouses with everything from ancient Buddha heads to Khmer sculptures. During art auctions in London this summer, two of the brightest sales were of prized Asian objects, both of them legitimately acquired: a Chinese Qianlong-era jade vase from a private collection that went for $280,000 at Bonham's and a calligraphy-brush washer from the Southern Song dynasty that sold for an astounding $1.2 million at Sotheby's.

The global appetite for such relics has sparked a lawless gold rush across Asia. In

"If you're bored one night, someone will say, 'Hey, let's go find a tomb.'"
—LITTLE SU,
former tomb raider

the past year alone, Indian police busted a smuggling ring that allegedly stripped hundreds of temples and monuments of sculptures and frescoes, then sent them on to be sold to collectors in the U.S. and Europe; Cambodian cops seized several truckloads of priceless Khmer sculptures crudely ripped from archaeological sites in Banteay Meanchey province; and Chinese officials uncovered the theft of 158 pieces of religious statuary from a collection lent to a museum in Chengde by the Forbidden City's Palace Museum in Beijing. Over the past five years, at least 220,000 ancient Chinese tombs have been broken into, according to estimates from China's National Cultural Relics Bureau.

The dramatic ransacking of Baghdad's national museum during the Iraq war may have grabbed headlines earlier this year, but the consistent, widespread and largely unremarked looting of Asia is far more damaging. "There is a feeling that Asia is filled with endless supplies of cultural relics," says He Shuzhong, head of Cultural Heritage Watch, a nongovernmental cultural-preservation group in Beijing. "But if the looting continues at this pace, we'll soon have nothing left to remind us of our glorious past. Baghdad was just a few weeks of destruction. Our heritage is experiencing a major blow every week, every month, every year."

No country has lost so much so quickly as Cambodia, whose jungles hid cities built by the mysterious Angkor Empire between the 9th and 14th centuries. Peace has proved far more destructive than war to the turbulent nation's antiquities. While the relic-rich northwest was under Khmer Rouge control through the mid-'90s, West-

SPECIALISTS
Xiaoli villagers make their own tools for raiding tombs

MARK LEONG—REDUX FOR TIME

1993 with the sole mission of protecting Cambodia's heritage. "Our history is so important to us that we have Angkor Wat on our flag," says Tranet. "So why are we as a people, as a government, as a country, allowing our heritage to slip through our fingers?"

On days when Tranet doesn't have much to do—and that's often, he admits, as he is hobbled by a lack of funding—he heads across town to the customs house in Phnom

losing the generous foreign aid provided by the diplomat's homeland.

For all his energy and passion, there's a sense of futility about Tranet's efforts. "Without a staff," he says, "I can only stop one person at a time. To do our job seriously, we need a big staff that checks every exit port every day." In the meantime, the industrial-scale looting continues unabated. In 1999 entire slabs of bas-relief from Banteay Chhmar, a magnificent temple in western Cambodia, were loaded onto trucks and driven to Thailand. Roads were bulldozed through the jungle to carry out the sandstone chunks, leading Thai police who later intercepted the load to charge the Cambodian military with complicity. This March looters trekked upriver to Kbal Spean, a distant jungle enclave where elaborately carved bas-reliefs from the 11th century decorate the riverbed and surrounding rocks. It was nighttime, and they found the site unguarded because of the lack of funds. Using an electric saw, the raiders gouged out the faces of the god Vishnu and his wife Lakshmi. Apparently, they were not experts: Lakshmi's face cleaved into several pieces, one of which was found beside the desecrated site the next day. Still Tranet estimates that the Vishnu face alone could sell for up to $50,000 in Bangkok—and several times that in the West.

No one has been arrested, and the local police just shake their heads when asked if an investigation is ongoing. Few will even

> ## "Baghdad was just a few weeks of destruction. Our heritage is experiencing a major blow every week, every month, every year."
> —HE SHUZHONG,
> Cultural Heritage Watch

ern dealers couldn't reach many of the prime sites for fear of land mines and cross fire. It was only with the full cessation of civil war a few years ago that foreigners could once again freely visit the relic sites around the legendary Angkor Wat temple complex. Since then, thousands of ancient Khmer relics have flooded the art market.

A diminutive, bowlegged archaeologist named Michel Tranet stands alone in trying to stanch that flow. Tranet is officially designated Undersecretary of State at Cambodia's Ministry of Culture and Fine Arts—but it's a comically grand title for a man whose entire staff consists of himself. Tranet, of Khmer-French parentage, returned from exile in

Penh. Earlier this year, Tranet prevented a Frenchman from bribing a customs official to let him leave with an 18th century Buddha stolen from a pagoda in Posat province. The 5.3-ft. wooden statue now stands in a backroom workshop at Cambodia's National Museum in Phnom Penh. If it were returned to the remote pagoda, Tranet fears that thieves would target it again. To Tranet, there are threats on every side—including foreign diplomats who use their immunity to sneak antiquities out of Cambodia without inspection. He suspects a Western diplomat has been smuggling objects overseas this way for more than a decade, while Cambodia's government has looked the other way, fearful of

A Xi'an gang broke into the 2,000-year-old tomb of China's Empress Dou and made off with a slew of rare artifacts. Here's how:

discuss the incident because in Cambodia corruption and bribery are endemic, and retribution can be severe for those who interfere in profitable criminal enterprises. "These are things we don't talk about," says Khieu Kort, a guard whose hammock hangs near the looted site. "It's too dangerous." Tranet is less circumspect. He blames the country's "chaotic political system," which encourages Cambodians to pillage, protected by local authorities who sometimes receive a piece of the action. "Last year [Cambodian Prime Minister] Hun Sen accused the West of stealing our culture," says Tranet, eyes blinking in agitation. "It's easy to blame the Westerners, but we're the ones who are handing over our culture to them."

To see how locals are plundering their heritage, travel to the desolate villages southeast of Xi'an, the city that is home to China's famed terra-cotta warriors. These villagers may be dirt poor, but the earth is rich. In early 2001 whispers began circulating that collectors would pay big money for anything dug up from the tomb of Empress Dou, a mighty dowager who died in 135 B.C. So well known was the burial site that locals assumed grave robbers had relieved the tomb's chambers of any gold or silver centuries ago. But now collectors were willing to pay for artifacts the farmers hadn't imagined anyone would want: clay pots grimy with antiquity, chipped ceramic statuettes and other detritus of burial rites. A local antiques dealer offered prospective tomb raiders $60 for a night's work—about the same amount the average local earns after taxes in a year.

Five villagers agreed to do the job. Using a *tangan*, a crude shovel with a specially curved blade and an extra-long handle, they probed deep into the earth around the mound, extracting core samples and examining the dirt for indicators such as traces of charcoal, which the ancients packed around tombs to ward off humidity. Locating a likely spot, the villagers lighted the fuse on a 110-lb. lump of homemade dynamite and blew a hole in the middle of a wheat field. Having blasted their way to a spot near the top of the tomb, they donned gas masks

1 Near Empress Dou's burial mound, raiders use a **TANGAN** to take soil samples, which indicate the exact location of the 131 ft. by 131 ft. tomb, buried deep underground

2 To speed up the digging, the gang blows out a crater at the surface with dynamite. They are careful not to set off the charge directly over the tomb—the impact might collapse the roof

3 A tunnel 115 ft. deep is excavated. The gang uses ropes to lower members and gear into the hole. An **AIR BLOWER** powered by a **PORTABLE GENERATOR** pumps in fresh air from the surface

4 To reach the tomb's roof, the raiders begin digging a 40-ft. spur tunnel at 98 ft. below

5 The raiders saw through the tomb's wood-plank roof. Wearing **GAS MASKS,** the gang now has access to the burial chamber—and all the treasures it contains

TOOLS OF THE TRADE

GAS MASKS Filter out stale air and noxious gases—built up during centuries of decay— inside the tomb

TANGAN This special shovel, which has a curved blade and steel screw-on handle extensions, can extract soil samples from 115 ft. below the earth's surface

AIR BLOWER An industrial electric fan pumps fresh air down the tunnel shaft to ventilate the burial chamber

PORTABLE GENERATOR The diesel-powered machine produces electricity to run fans and lights

Imperial gravediggers surround tombs with charcoal and dried mud for protection against moisture

Coffin

Statues symbolize the servants, soldiers and maidens who served the royals in life

Only cypress wood was used, probably for its ability to absorb water

131 ft.

131 ft.

EMPRESS DOU'S GRAVE

Empress Dou's coffin is surrounded by a wooden structure called *huangchang ticou*, a burial method reserved for Han dynasty emperors and their wives and concubines

Drawing is not to scale
TIME Graphic by Dennis Wong and Cecelia Wong
Text by Kate Drake
Sources: Xi'an Municipal Public Securities Bureau; Shaanxi Archaeology Research Institute; China's Buried Kingdoms (TIME-LIFE Books)

QILAI SHEN FOR TIME (4)

to filter out the stale tomb air, then tunneled into the burial chamber.

By the next morning, the acrid smell of explosives had wafted to the nearest village, and someone tipped off the cops that looters might be at work. The following night police staked out the tomb. Three raiders were caught; two got away. State press reports hailed the arrests as a triumph, but instead of filling in the hole and posting a guard, the underfunded local cultural-relics bureau simply placed wooden planks across the hole and tossed in some dirt. Before long, other gangs pilfered at least 200 treasures, mostly ceramic statues, from the site. Among the loveliest of these pieces was a series of delicately painted female figurines, which could fetch at least $10,000 in the Xi'an underground market and up to $80,000 in London or New York City. Though just as rare, other figurines from Empress Dou's tomb were worth only $6,000 apiece because of their unprepossessing color, a charcoal gray unique to some ceramics of this region.

To the destitute farmers of central China, the allure of such plunder is hard to resist—but the reality of life as a tomb raider is less enticing. Feng, who asks to be identified only by his last name, recalls vividly the first time he descended into the crumbly earth of Henan province six years ago. In his village on the outskirts of Luoyang, robbing a tomb is similar to an initiation rite, and Feng, then 19, was filled with nervous excitement as he and a group of fellow raiders ambled into a local wheat field to see what they could dig up. It was after midnight, and they had been drinking. In truth, Feng admits, he was a little spooked—children in this area are raised on ghost stories of imperial ancestors, haunting mischievous villagers. As the men tossed up spadefuls of dirt, chatting and laughing under the glare of a light hooked up to a generator, Feng noticed a smell he likened to fermented bean curd.

A few minutes later, Feng's uncle told him that as the youngest, he would have the honor of going down on a solo reconnaissance mission. Eager to prove himself, Feng slithered down into the darkness with only a rope as a guide. But upon reaching the floor of the tomb, he was overwhelmed by the smell. Feng remembers nothing after that. Later his uncle told him he had fainted from the putrid air and had to be dragged out. The operation was halted until the next night when the looters lugged in an industrial air blower to clear out the tomb. After his uncle and another villager emerged with the first of five Tang-dynasty ceramic animals—each worth about $10,000 in the West—the young Feng felt a touch of propri-

etary pride. "I risked my life for those statues," he says. "But when they came up with such expensive things, I was hooked." Feng, who was paid $45 for his maiden raid, doesn't mention the pieces' beauty. It's beyond him why Westerners would waste so much money on them. But the thrill of the treasure hunt hasn't diminished: "The excitement gives our lives some meaning."

Of course, his chosen field is not without its risks. Middlemen and dealers, who receive a vastly larger share of the profits from stolen art, are rarely prosecuted for their crimes. But the authorities occasionally like to make an example of the lowly looters, who are easier to catch. Last year Chinese courts meted out death penalties to at least four tomb raiders. "I know someone who was executed for looting a tomb," says Feng. "He made 580 yuan [$70]. Now, I hear the tricolor female statue he dug up was recently resold in New York for 150,000 yuan [$18,000]. No one is getting arrested in New York. How fair is that?"

Once in a great while, though, a big fish does get caught. For years Indian police suspected unassuming handicrafts trader Vaman Narayan Ghia of leading a massive antiques-smuggling network that robbed hundreds of temples and palaces of their finest treasures. But the graying 55-year-old had always been far too careful to allow any cracks in his operation, police say. Each member of his art-smuggling chain knew only the member directly above, making it nearly impossible to connect the thieves who were occasionally caught with stolen art to the mastermind at the top. But on June 6, after an intense, yearlong operation involving scores of police, the Indian authorities believed they had the proof to link two stolen statues to Ghia. Still, as police knocked on the door of Ghia's house in Jaipur to arrest him, they had no idea they were on the verge of dismantling the largest antiquities-smuggling ring in India's modern history.

Inside Ghia's home, the cops say they found hundreds of photographs of looted 9th to 11th century statues, a long list of private collectors' phone numbers and 68 auction-house catalogs featuring some of the same artifacts. Based on a detailed confession from Ghia, police claim he spent 30 years smuggling an estimated 50,000 idols, paintings and statues stolen from protected monuments around the country. On Sept. 2, charges were filed against Ghia and 21 alleged looters believed to be part of his smuggling ring. Police retrieved stolen goods from some of them, including a dismantled

Moving th

To New York City

Switzerland
Lacks stiff documentation requirements for goods moving through customs, creating an ideal transit port for laundering illicit art

AFRICA

THE LEFT FOOT OF ZEUS

① Kabul, Afghanistan
French archaeologists excavate this 11-inch long marble carving at the Ai Khanum ruins in 1968. It goes on display at the Kabul Museum until 1993, when it is stolen

② Peshawar, Pakistan
The foot is purchased by a Japanese antiques dealer in 2000

③ Tokyo
Two years later, the dealer decides to entrust UNESCO with the piece until it may be returned safely to Afghanistan. Today the foot is traveling around Japan as part of a museum display

Big Business

Asia's stolen-art trade is carried ou on an almost industrial scale

220,000
tombs in China have been broken into over the past five years

REMAINS: Bones get left behind

Loot
Recent busts of smuggling rackets shed light on the black-market trade routes of Asia's stolen art

RUSSIA

London
Like New York City, it is a major consumer of antiquities, but tighter controls have curtailed some illegal trade

Hong Kong
Some galleries on Hollywood Road furtively sell items stolen from the mainland

To New York City

Kabul ① ②

Xi'an ①

New York City
A wealth of auction houses, galleries, museums and collectors makes it a key destination for Asian artifacts

Udaipur ①

③

②

Sisophon ①

INDIAN OCEAN

Bangkok
Its antiques shops offer many purloined Cambodian relics

②

PACIFIC OCEAN

INDONESIA

CLOCKWISE FROM TOP LEFT: PROFESSOR IKUO HIRAYAMA—UNESCO; JOHN STANMEYER—VII FOR TIME; PENG ZHANGQING—XINHUA; WANG GANG—IMAGINECHINA

DANCING LADIES

① Udaipur, India
According to Indian police, confessed smuggler Vaman Narayan Ghia removes four sculptures from the ceiling of the Saas Bahu temple in November 1999 and six months later, another four

② Switzerland
To cover his tracks, Ghia allegedly ships two of the pieces through Europe before routing them to their final stop in the U.S.

③ New York City
A Manhattan gallery owner publishes photographs of two of the statues in a 2002 catalog

BAS-RELIEF BUDDHA

① Sisophon, Cambodia
In January 1999 looters cut away a bas-relief frieze from the Banteay Chhmar temple and load all 117 pieces onto trucks

② Cambodia-Thailand border
Before entering Thailand the thieves hire a vehicle normally used to transport water buffalo to sneak the goods into Bangkok. They are intercepted by Thai police but escape; the frieze is returned

TERRA-COTTA STATUES

① Xi'an, China
In 2001 grave robbers steal figurines from a 2,000-year-old tomb and sell some for about $36 each

② Hong Kong
A Hollywood Road art dealer admits he bought 32 of the relics from a middleman

③ New York City
Sotheby's schedules six of the statuettes for a March 2002 auction. Estimated value: $6,000 to $8,000 each. After the Chinese government protests, the figurines are returned to Xi'an

98%
of profits from the illicit art trade go to middlemen and dealers

Vaman Narayan Ghia, the alleged king of Indian-antiques theft, is accused of smuggling some **50,000** relics stolen over the past 30 years

◀ The security chief at a museum in Chengde, China, was accused in June of stealing 158 artifacts over 12 years. One, the Buddha of Infinite Life, fetched

$295,000
at an auction in Hong Kong last October

Indian police estimate that only

2%
of the country's antiquities thefts are reported

Illicit sales of Afghan relics are outpacing the **$1.2 billion-a-year** opium trade

Up to 75% of all antiquities offered for sale in London auctions have no published provenance

ENFORCER Although Tranet runs a one-man operation as protector of Cambodia's ancient treasures, he managed to stop a French tourist from smuggling this 18th century Buddha out of the country

Mughal pavilion the size of a small house and a 9.8-ft. Buddha statue that had been broken into three parts to ease transportation. Several of Ghia's foreign clients have been named in the police charge sheet, and Indian police will seek authorization through the Foreign Ministry to question them. "We have enough evidence to prepare several cases against these people," says Jaipur superintendent Anand Shrivastava, who is heading the investigation.

In one case, according to police, Ghia confessed to sending the owners of a Manhattan gallery some photographs of a temple ceiling adorned with 16 statues. The gallery owners agreed on a price, police say, and Ghia then arranged for the statues to be stolen and sent to the buyers in New York City. In his lengthy written confession, Ghia stated that other private collectors and dealers came to India and toured deserted temples to pick out precisely what they wanted stolen for them.

Some items that Ghia allegedly stole ended up on the block in Sotheby's and Christie's auction houses, say Indian authorities. Relics listed in Christie's catalogs that police say were taken by Ghia included a 2.6-ft. sandstone frieze with an estimated value of $200,000 to $300,000 and a 2.7-ft. statue of the Hindu god Shiva. A Jain statue that was reported stolen on Oct. 7, 1999, turned up as Lot 135 in a Sotheby's September 2000 catalog.

It's entirely possible, however, that the auction houses and galleries did not know the items were stolen. "Christie's are in contact with authorities and are helping them with their inquiries," said a spokesperson for Christie's London office. "As the investigation is ongoing, we do not have any further information to release at this time." Diana Phillips, senior vice president at Sotheby's, says, "We have not knowingly sold any items consigned by Mr. Ghia or companies affiliated with him for the past several years." Sotheby's, says Phillips, does not offer for sale "any object that we know or suspect is stolen, smuggled or looted."

One of the private gallery owners with whom Ghia claims to have done business, according to Indian police, is Arnold Lieberman, one of America's foremost dealers in Asian antiquities. When contacted, Lieberman said he had never met Ghia. "I'm a known person [in the industry]," he said (and thus an easy target). Mother-daughter Manhattan dealers Doris and Nancy Wiener were also named by Ghia. Nancy Wiener said she knew nothing about the case or Ghia. According-

ing to an art-world source, Ghia's arrest sent shock waves through the business.

The very nature of antiquities makes the issue of ownership particularly murky. Many countries now have laws banning the export of ancient treasures, and an item taken recently from a temple or a grave or a palace is, by definition, stolen—but stolen from whom? Though much of European art sold by reputable dealers tends to have a detailed provenance—a record of where and when the item was procured and how it changed hands—antiquities from the developing world are often not held to the same standards. Only a tiny percentage of stolen art is ever reported. Indeed, hundreds of thousands of artifacts have yet to be documented by overburdened cultural-relics officials, so no paper trail exists.

Furthermore, in ancient civilizations such as India and China, some spoils of war and colonialism purloined a century or two ago by invaders have gradually come to be considered the legitimate property of whoever possesses them. Many international dealers and auction houses argue that Asia's turbulent history makes it simply impossible for them to track the chain of ownership. But He, from Beijing-based Cultural Heritage Watch, says dealers aren't trying hard enough and adds, "Can you imagine a Renoir suddenly appearing on the international market without any history of where it came from? It's outrageous that nobody gives

BIG FISH Ghia was arrested by Indian police at his home after a yearlong investigation. His alleged antiquities-smuggling ring is the largest in India's modern history

Asian art the same scrutiny." An art dealer in Hong Kong is equally blunt about the benefits of willful ignorance. "Once these goods are taken from their original source, you can't prove they were stolen," he says. "It's as if they never existed at all."

Nevertheless, isolated victories do occur, as in the case of some of the figurines looted from Empress Dou's tomb. By February 2002, the Xi'an police had caught Wang Cangyan, a local dealer who oversaw the shipment of dozens of Empress Dou's figurines to Hong Kong, sneaking them through customs checkpoints by hiding them inside a truckload of new ceramics. Wang told the Xi'an police the name of a Hong Kong shop to which he had sold 32 statuettes.

Packed with legitimate antiques shops and those that specialize in fakes, Hong Kong's Hollywood Road is a key Asian transit point for stolen Chinese antiquities. The rarest items are seldom displayed. "If someone walks in off the street and asks to see some real antiques, I'll probably show them fakes," says a Hollywood Road dealer who declines to be named. "But if they come in knowing exactly what they want and they know what the market rate is, I'll bring in the real things from my warehouse." In 2001, this dealer—who was busted a few years ago for selling an illicit item that was later impounded in the U.S.— heard about a collection of figurines stolen from Empress Dou's tomb. He says he tried to get his hands on them, but another gallery owner, just down the street, scored the statues instead. In retrospect, he says, "I'm glad I didn't get to buy them. I don't need any more trouble."

For Wang Cangyan, the dealer who had arranged the smuggling of the 32 figurines to Hong Kong, there has been plenty of trouble. He is currently serving a jail sentence, albeit significantly reduced to two years in return for his cooperation with the authorities. As for the Hong Kong gallery that bought the figurines from Wang: it was allowed to return them quietly to the mainland in exchange for keeping its identity secret.

But several of the other figurines that were smuggled to Hong Kong proved more elusive. The Xi'an police believe they were sneaked out of Hong Kong into Switzerland, where strict export documentation isn't required. From there, say the police, they made their way to New York City. Tang Xiaojin, the Xi'an cop charged with tracking down the figurines, discovered this by accident when he was leafing through a copy of the March 2002 catalog *Fine Chinese Ceramics and Works of Art* from Sotheby's. Flipping past treasure after treasure, Tang suddenly stopped. Lot 32, credited as belonging to "various owners," was very familiar: six charcoal gray figurines that were part of the very loot Tang had been tracking for months. They were set to go on sale in New York City in

PRIZE PORKER This pig statue, stolen in India, went to market but was later recovered, allegedly from some of Ghia's associates

just a few days' time. "I was astonished," recalls Tang. "I never imagined they would have made it all the way to America."

Tang and his colleagues moved fast. The Chinese embassy in Washington dispatched a representative to the auction house's New York office. At first, according to a Chinese diplomat, Sotheby's refused to exclude Lot 32 from auction, saying the Chinese didn't have enough proof that the items had been taken from an imperial tomb just months before. Phillips, the Sotheby's spokeswoman, says it had an unequivocal written warranty stating that the owner had good title to the objects. She also noted that none of the statuettes appeared in the Art Loss Registry, an international database of stolen art, which Sotheby's co-founded. The only indication the auction house had that they were illicit came via a written request from China's ambassador, Phillips says. After a flurry of negotiations, the auction house pulled the items—just 20 minutes before the bidding was set to begin.

Now, more than a year later, the six statuettes have been returned to China. They're currently on show at a tatty museum on the outskirts of Xi'an in a display proudly titled "The Special Exhibition of Returned Pottery Figures of Western Han Dynasty from America." Pointedly, each statuette still has a tag from Sotheby's attached to its feet. Li Ku, vice director of the museum, rejoices in the figurines' return. "Looking at these figures, I feel like my family has come home at last," he says.

But, in truth, much of the loot from Empress Dou's tomb—and the vast majority from countless other sites across Asia—is still missing. In India, Superintendent Shrivastava is delighted to have nabbed the nation's top smuggler. But months after the momentous arrest, he has tracked down only a fraction of the relics Ghia is believed to have looted over the past three decades. Since news of the arrest was made public, three collectors have written to the police, offering to return stolen items they say they purchased in good faith. But most of the stolen treasures, still hidden inside a Manhattan loft or a Hong Kong boardroom, will probably never be recovered. "There is plenty," Shrivastava mourns, "that has been lost forever." —**With reporting by Bu Hua/Xi'an, Simon Crittle/ New York, Meenakshi Ganguly/ Jaipur, Aparisim Ghosh/London and Robert Horn/Bangkok**

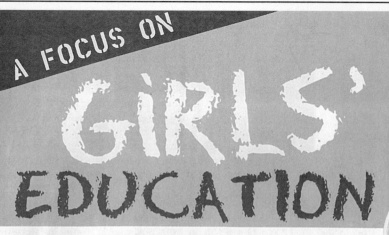

A FOCUS ON GiRLS' EDUCATION

Meena, a popular cartoon character, teaches kids in Bangladesh that boys and girls are equal.

©UNICEF/GRO-03/Frederick

BANGLADESH

Over 121 million children don't go to school. Almost 65 million of them are girls

All children should have equal rights, but in many parts of the world, girls do not have the same rights as boys. In Bangladesh, one of the poorest countries in the world, many girls receive smaller portions at meal-times than their brothers. In some nations, such as Bolivia, girls often stay at home to care for younger brothers or sisters, do household chores or work in the fields. In India, some families send only their sons to school. And schools in many African countries charge high prices, forcing poor families to choose which of their children will be educated.

25 BY 2005: UNICEF IN ACTION

Working to get more girls into schools, UNICEF started the 25 by 2005 program. It hopes to increase the number of girls in school in 25 countries by 2005. Fifteen of these countries, including Sudan and Chad, are in Africa, and six, including Bangladesh and India, are in south Asia. Other countries include Bolivia and Turkey. UNICEF chose these nations because fewer girls than boys go to school in them, and because each of the countries has more than 1 million girls out of school.

In Bolivia, a mountainous South American country, many people live in rural areas where there are few schools. UNICEF is working to help build local schools so kids won't have to travel far. And to make schools more welcoming to girls, UNICEF is helping to make them clean and safe by building separate bathrooms for boys and girls.

To teach children and adults in Bangladesh that boys and girls have equal rights, UNICEF is using a popular cartoon character named Meena. Over 6.3 million schoolchildren read about her adventures or see her on television every day. Meena's message: Boys and girls can do the same things. People are starting to listen and to pay attention to that simple message. And that's good news for everyone!

—By Jackie Wlodarczak

Education is changing the lives of kids in Bolivia.

BOLIVIA

©Anders Ryman/CORBIS

www.unicefusa.org/youthaction

Girls Speak Out!

"My mother has suffered very much in her life. My dream is to be able to tell her she doesn't have to worry anymore, because I'll look after her. If I could go again to school, it might help."
Sumi, 11 years old, Bangladesh

"My dream is to become a doctor. But dreams remain dreams. . . . School is only free up to this year."
Jasmine, 13 years old, Bangladesh

"Before, it was harder for girls to go to school and it wasn't easy for them to finish, because they had to work. I think that is changing because everyone in the community understands how important it is to have an education."
Liliana, 8 years old, Bolivia

"Usually I get up at 5:00 A.M. to fetch water for breakfast. There is no water here, but a truck comes a couple of times a week to fill a container at the end of the road. It's not far, but it gets heavy. I also have to help my mother with chores before I go to school. . . . I feel lucky, because my parents didn't have the chance to go to school when they were young."
Francisca, 12 years old, Bolivia

Give two reasons some girls do not go to school. What is UNICEF doing to get more girls into school?

Meet UNICEF

UNICEF, the United Nations Children's Fund, is an organization that helps children in 158 countries and territories. Every day in some part of the world, UNICEF programs deliver food supplies, clean water, vaccines to protect people from diseases, school supplies and emergency relief to children and their families.

For over 50 years, U.S. kids have been trick-or-treating for UNICEF. Young people are holding bake sales, read-a-thons and car washes to raise money to help children in other countries.

In this *TFK Extra!* you'll learn about some of the important programs and places where UNICEF is helping others. And you'll meet youth leaders who are encouraging others to learn about UNICEF and to take action to improve kids' lives around the globe.

Meet T.J.

NANCY DANIELS

NAME: T.J. Daniels
AGE: 12

What he did: organized a schoolwide Trick-or-Treat for UNICEF campaign

After reading last year's *TFK Extra!* T.J. decided he didn't want just to read about the challenges kids are facing in the world. He wanted to help them! So he asked his teacher and his principal if his school could take part in Trick-or-Treat for UNICEF. The answer was yes! T.J. was asked to lead the effort.

First, he gave a presentation about UNICEF at a school assembly. Then he passed out UNICEF trick-or-treat boxes along with a flyer that explained the program. T.J. and his classmates raised $1,325.

T.J. says, "I hope that my work will inspire others to start a UNICEF program at their school so we can continue to help those who are less fortunate."

Around the World with UNICEF!

The map below shows some of the places where UNICEF is working. Learn more about UNICEF and these countries as you read your *TFK Extra!*

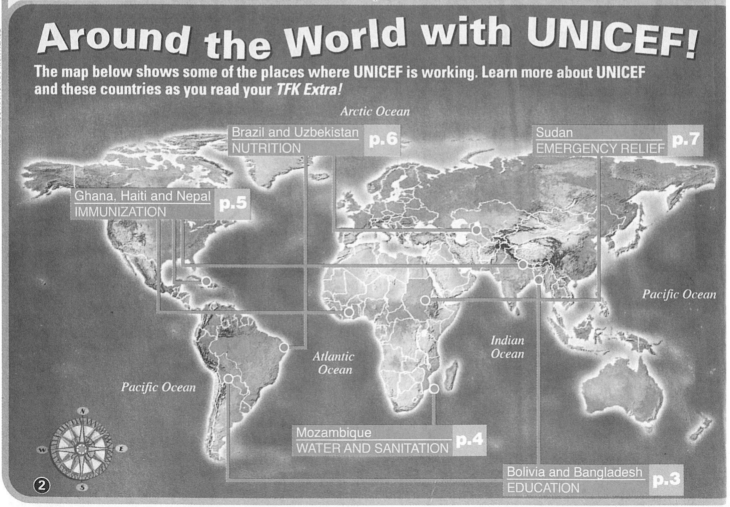

MAP ILLUSTRATION BY RICK NEASE

Arctic Ocean

Brazil and Uzbekistan
NUTRITION **p.6**

Sudan
EMERGENCY RELIEF **p.7**

Ghana, Haiti and Nepal
IMMUNIZATION **p.5**

Pacific Ocean

Atlantic Ocean

Indian Ocean

Pacific Ocean

Mozambique
WATER AND SANITATION **p.4**

Bolivia and Bangladesh
EDUCATION **p.3**

②

exit
u-nu-go-s-di
ᎤᏄᎪᏍᏗ

▲ Objects at the school, like this sign, are labeled with Cherokee words.

◄ In music class, second, third and fourth graders sing Cherokee songs.

COVER STORY
Saving Their Native Language

Walk past the music room at Lost City School near Hulbert, Oklahoma. You will hear some unusual sounds! The kids shout that Old MacDonald had a *wa-ga* and a *ka-wo-nu* on his farm. The words mean "cow" and "duck" in **Cherokee.**

In the building next door, kindergarten kids learn everything from colors to numbers in Cherokee. They are called by their **Native** Indian names. The kids speak only in Cherokee for most of the day. They are the first public school students to do this in the United States.

Why Learn the Language?

Cherokee is one of 170 or so Native Indian languages in the U.S. All of the languages are in danger of disappearing. About 99 out of every 100 people who can speak and understand Cherokee well are over the age of 45.

"If we don't learn Cherokee, our grandsons won't know it," says Crystal Braden, 13. Lost

▲ A Cherokee leader told students a Native story about animals.

City School has 100 students. Crystal is one of the 65 students who are Cherokee. Her class just finished making a video to teach Cherokee words for colors to younger students.

Kristian Smith, 10, is learning words from his little brother, Lane, who is in kindergarten. "It's weird," says Kristian. "I'm the one who should be teaching him!"

The Cherokee word *ga-du-gi* describes the school's work. It means "working together to help the community." November is National American Indian Heritage Month. But at Lost City School, everyone works together all year long.

WHAT'S THE SCOOP?

Why is it important for kids to learn American Indian languages?

PHOTOGRAPHS BY KELLY KERR FOR TIME FOR KIDS

TIME FOR KIDS

COVER STORY

In Russia, former hunters now help protect the big cats.

TiGERS ROAR BACK

One hundred thousand tigers **roamed** Asia in 1900. By 1994, that number had dropped to 7,000. Experts warned that the big cats would be **extinct** by 2000.

The world took the warning seriously. Working to save the cats has become a way of life in many Asian countries. Last month, tiger experts gathered in Washington, D.C., to hear a new report from the Save the Tiger Fund. The good news: Tiger **populations** have stopped shrinking!

"The tiger survives today thanks to hard work and public support," says John Seidensticker, the head of Save the Tiger.

In southeastern Russia, 350 to 400 Siberian tigers survive. That is almost a miracle. From 1990 to 1993, illegal hunters killed one-third of all Siberian tigers!

Now a program hires the former hunters to help protect the cats. At the region's Tiger Day festivals, kids dress in stripes and whiskers to celebrate their pride in helping the cats survive.

In India, tigers share their **habitat** with humans. A program is helping some Indians find homes outside tiger habitats. Volunteers lead the project. Conservationist Ullas Karanth says local people are the key to saving tigers. "Their **commitment**," he says, "can't be bought with money." ■

Bengal tigers, like this mom and cub, can also be white.

What steps have helped save tigers? What else can be done to protect them?

DID YOU KNOW?

RUSSIA

Siberian tigers
350 – 400

Bengal tigers
3,200 – 4,500

CHINA

South China tigers
20 – 30

INDIA

Indochinese tigers
1,200 – 1,800

BANGLADESH

Pacific Ocean

Sumatran tigers
400 – 500

INDONESIA

Indian Ocean

Tigers, the world's biggest cats, are found only in Asia.

Tigers are divided into five groups or subspecies (see map).

Tiger stripes are like human fingerprints. No two tigers have the same pattern of stripes.

Tiger cubs weigh two to three pounds at birth and are born blind.

Tigers live 10 to 15 years in the wild.

Tigers can leap up to 30 feet.

TIME FOR KIDS

Testing, Testing . . .

Paige Donahoo is scared and a bit excited as she waits for April to arrive. That's when she and all the other third graders in Texas will take their first special reading and math tests. "I don't skip any school because I might miss test practice," says Paige.

Soon, every third grader in the U.S. will face such tests. So will older kids. President Bush signed the No Child Left Behind Act this month. By 2005, kids in grades three through eight will be taking reading and math tests every year. Each state will decide what students need to learn to pass the tests.

A 7-year-old student tackles a big test.

Why More Tests?

Fans of the new law believe testing is the best way to see how well kids—and schools—are doing. The law also gives more money and help to schools in poorer areas.

Some people worry that teachers will spend too much time preparing kids for the tests, leaving less time for other subjects. Last year, Tessa Wooden of Venice, California, and her second-grade classmates had to practice for their tests during gym!

State tests will be a fact of life for kids, so check out the tips below. "Keep calm," advises James Tyrrell, 9. "Just try the best you can."

—*By Elizabeth Siris*

 Find out what kids are saying about testing at *timeforkids.com/testing*

Bush greets kids after a speech on the new education law. "We're bringing new resources to struggling schools," he said.

What advice would you give classmates to help them during a big test?

Tips for Test Time

See how many of these helpful tips you already follow when you have a big test.

1) Eat a healthy breakfast before your test.
2) Read the directions carefully. Ask your teacher for help if you don't understand.
3) Take a deep breath and focus. Don't panic!
4) If you don't know an answer, skip the question and come back to it later.
5) Check over your answers to make sure you marked the correct choice.

The Average Number of Thunderstorm Days in a Year

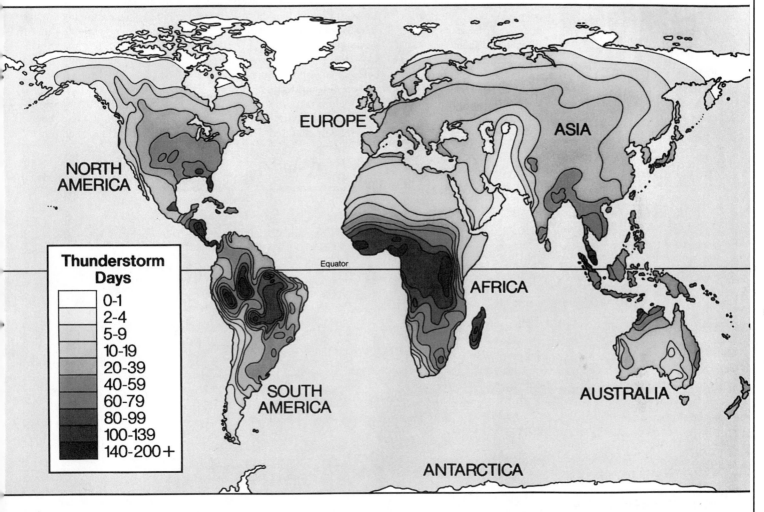

Thunderstorm Days
- 0-1
- 2-4
- 5-9
- 10-19
- 20-39
- 40-59
- 60-79
- 80-99
- 100-139
- 140-200+

NORTH AMERICA

EUROPE

ASIA

Equator

AFRICA

SOUTH AMERICA

AUSTRALIA

ANTARCTICA

SUMMER OF THE SHARK

Sharks don't really like to bite people. A great white shark prefers to eat a seal. A bull shark loves fish and even another shark! Then why was this summer full of scary news about shark attacks? Scientists say that is one good question.

Last year sharks bit 84 people worldwide. This year there have been 52 attacks so far. Most were in Florida.

One reason for the high numbers is that more people are in the ocean than ever before. Many splash around in the morning and early evening. That's when sharks hunt.

Sharks that attack humans are probably confused. They might mistake a human foot for a fish. "Sharks are not out to get humans," says scientist Dr. Robert Lea. "It is just humans sharing a spot in the ocean with sharks at the wrong time."

Don't panic. The odds of being attacked by a shark are slim. You are 30 times more likely to be hit by lightning!

Super-sharp senses let sharks see, hear and smell underwater

Learn more about sharks at www.timeforkids.com/sharks

EYES Like cats, sharks can see well in dim light.

EARS Holes on the shark's head lead to its ears. Sharks might hear a fish swimming 600 yards away.

NOSE Sharks can smell underwater. Smell is one of their sharpest senses.

SKIN A shark's skin is made of scales that look like tiny, pointed teeth. A row of special sensors in the shark's skin help it track down small fish.

THE WHOLE TOOTH The great white shark in this picture has teeth this size!

Graphic for TIME by Ed Gabel
Source for the Top 5: Top 10 of Everything 2001, DK Publishing

WHAT'S THE SCOOP?

Sharks were alive when dinosaurs roamed the earth. Why do you think sharks have been around for so long?

TOP 5 HEAVIEST SHARKS

There are at least 370 different kinds of sharks. They can be 6 inches to 40 feet long. Here are the five heaviest:

1 **WHALE SHARK:** 46,300 pounds

2 **BASKING SHARK:** 32,000 pounds

3 **GREAT WHITE SHARK:** 7,300 pounds

4 **GREENLAND SHARK:** 2,250 pounds

5 **TIGER SHARK:** 2,070 pounds

TIME FOR KIDS   SEPTEMBER 14, 2001

"The *Eagle* Has Landed"

The *Eagle* sped toward the surface of the moon at more than 3,000 miles (4,800 kilometers) per hour. Armstrong and Aldrin stood side by side, tethered to the floor by elastic cords. While Armstrong looked out the window and piloted the lunar module, Aldrin kept his eyes on the computer and other onboard instruments. Suddenly, at 3,000 feet (923 meters), warning lights flashed on the control panel, and high-pitched alarms rang in their headsets. But Mission Control quickly informed the astronauts that their computer had become overloaded, trying to process too much data too fast. Nothing was wrong with the lunar module, and it was safe to continue with the landing.

Aldrin kept reading out the data: "Seven hundred feet [210 meters]," he said, giving their altitude above the surface. "Down at twenty-one," he added, meaning they were descending at twenty-one feet (six meters) per second. "Six hundred feet [180 meters], down at nineteen [five meters]."

Armstrong could see the landing site their navigation system was steering them toward, and he didn't like what he saw. A crater the size of a football field was directly in their path, and it was surrounded by boulders, some of them as big as cars. The *Eagle* could be ripped apart if he put it down there. Armstrong took over manual control of the lunar module, slowed down the rate of descent, and skimmed over the crater. As the moon's battered surface loomed closer and closer, Armstrong searched urgently for a better landing spot. Aldrin continued in a steady voice: "One hundred feet [thirty meters], three-and-a-half [one meter] down. Five percent fuel remaining. Quantity light." "Light" meant that they had only sixty seconds of fuel left.

None of Aldrin's practice runs (left) prepared him for the drama of the actual moon landing (opposite).

Out of time, Armstrong finally spotted a flat area and set the *Eagle* down in billowing gusts of moon dust. Armstrong and Aldrin grinned at each other through their bubble helmets, then reached out and shook hands.

"Iceberg! Right Ahead!"

By the time these words rang out on the RMS *Titanic,* it was too late. The warning came at 11:40 p.m. on the clear, cold night of April 14, 1912, in the icy seas of the North Atlantic. Within 40 seconds, the ship's starboard (right) side was raked below the waterline by the submerged spur of an iceberg. Less than three hours later, the *Titanic* sank beneath the water. At least 1,523 of its roughly 2,228

CHECK IT OUT!

Where does the name RMS *Titanic* come from?

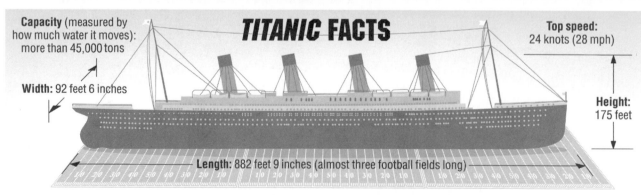

TITANIC FACTS

Capacity (measured by how much water it moves): more than 45,000 tons

Width: 92 feet 6 inches

Top speed: 24 knots (28 mph)

Height: 175 feet

Length: 882 feet 9 inches (almost three football fields long)

2

passengers and crew were dead or dying.

Had the *Titanic* missed the iceberg that Sunday, it may have simply been remembered as one of the largest, most luxurious ocean liners of its time. Yet so much went wrong that the *Titanic* has become a symbol for disaster. The great ship's story is a drama with a little of everything: heroism and fear, humility and arrogance, wealth and poverty, life and death.

Come aboard the grand ship for a voyage of a lifetime—from the safety of home.

◄ ON THE NIGHT it sank, the *Titanic* was making its maiden (first) voyage across the Atlantic Ocean.

FATAL FLAWS

The rivets (metal bolts used to join steel plates) on the TITANIC contained metallic impurities. As a result, the rivet heads tended to pop off when the ship scraped the iceberg. Once a rivet head popped, the seams between plates separated, and water entered the ship.

3

Building a Colossus

Boats have been around from the time of our earliest ancestors. Boats enabled people to cross wide rivers and fish in deep waters. As people began to explore distant lands, they found better ways to build larger and stronger boats.

Around A.D. 1000, Viking explorers from Norway, Sweden, and Denmark sailed to North America in wooden boats no bigger than today's mobile homes. But traveling the Atlantic then—and for centuries afterward—was dangerous. Icebergs, storms, poor navigational equip-

A Floating Mastodon

Viking Longship	Mayflower	USS *Constitution*	RMS *Titanic*
Raiding vessel	Merchant ship	Frigate	Ocean liner
Built around A.D. 1000	Built in 1610	Built in 1797	Built in 1911
65–90 feet long	106 feet long	204 feet long	882 feet 9 inches long
30–60 passengers	120 passengers	500 passengers	3,547 passengers

TITANIC TIME LINE

1908 The White Star Line approves plans for three of the biggest ocean liners in history. They will be called *Olympic, Titanic,* and *Gigantic.* Construction begins on *Olympic.*

1909 Construction begins on the *Titanic* in Belfast, Northern Ireland.

4

ment, and unreliable sail power cost thousands of people their lives, as did disease and unsanitary conditions.

By the late 1800s, transatlantic crossings had become more routine. Ships were now powered by steam engines and built of iron and steel. (*Ship* is the term used for a large seagoing vessel.)

Shipping companies began building giant ocean liners. In the early 1900s, the White Star Line was in a heated race with competitors to build even bigger, more impressive ships. In 1912, after three years under construction, the largest moving object in the world— the *Titanic*—was unveiled.

THE DIRECTOR

THE DESIGNER

▲ **J. BRUCE ISMAY** was managing director of the White Star Line and a driving force in the creation of the *Titanic*. Ismay was on board the *Titanic* during its maiden voyage and escaped the sinking ship in one of the *Titanic*'s collapsible lifeboats, perhaps thinking that his testimony would be valuable later. However, his reputation suffered after the tragedy. He was accused of saving himself while the captain and others died.

▲ **THOMAS ANDREWS** was the *Titanic*'s designer. He was famous for knowing every detail of

the ship. He listened carefully to crew members' complaints and made changes when possible. Andrews sailed on the *Titanic* to identify the problems that always come up in a brand-new ship. Like the captain, Andrews perished.

➤ **THE *TITANIC*'S** captain, Edward J. Smith, was often called the "millionaires' captain" because wealthy families asked to book passage on his ships. The White Star Line made him captain of the *Olympic* and later of the *Titanic*. In two years, he was to command the *Gigantic* on its maiden run. He did not survive.

AT LEFT ARE THE propellers of *Titanic*'s sister ship *Olympic*. (There are no photographs of the *Titanic*'s propellers.) It took three thousand men three years to build the *Titanic*. The work was done in Belfast, Northern Ireland, at the Harland & Queen's Island Shipyards.

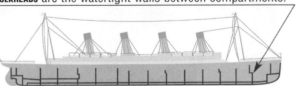

BULKHEADS are the watertight walls between compartments.

▲ THE *TITANIC* could float if any two of her 16 "watertight" compartments flooded, or even if the first four flooded.

However, if the first five sections flooded, the bow (front) would sink so low that the water in the fifth compartment

would overflow into the sixth, and when that section filled, water would overflow into the seventh, and so on.

FATAL FLAWS

The British technical journal THE SHIPBUILDER was so impressed with TITANIC's bulkheads (left) and other safety features that it pronounced the ship "practically unsinkable." However, the bulkheads rose only 10 feet above the waterline. Had they been built higher, the ship might not have sunk.

1910 *Olympic* launched (set afloat).

1911 *Titanic* launched. White Star Line continues with changes and improvements that make it the largest ship in the world (left). *Olympic* makes its maiden voyage.

5

The Classes of 1912

People in 1912 were very aware of their class, or position, in society. Class was determined by family background, wealth, and education, among other things. On the *Titanic*, the price of a passenger's ticket said a lot about that person's position in society.

WHITE STAR LINE
ROYAL & UNITED STATES MAIL STEAMERS

FIRST CLASS ★★★ **TICKET PRICE: $1,500 to $4,350** ($26,741 to $77,549 in today's money)

➤ **THE WHITE STAR** Line spared no expense to make its first-class rooms as opulent as possible. They came complete with thick carpets and overstuffed sofas and chairs. First-class passengers had at their disposal a gymnasium, swimming pool, squash court, Turkish bath, and library.

FIRST-CLASS STAIRCASE

➤ **THE PRESS CALLED** the *Titanic* the "millionaires' special" because there were so many wealthy people traveling first-class. Their combined fortunes were around $500 million ($9 billion today). Among the rich and famous people were the following:

JOHN JACOB ASTOR, New York millionaire, and wife **MADELEINE** (He died; she survived.)

ARCHIBALD BUTT Military adviser to President William Howard Taft (He died.)

ISIDOR AND IDA STRAUS He was a founder of Macy's department store. (Both died.)

Scotland's **LUCY NOELLE MARTHA DYER-EDWARDS, THE COUNTESS OF ROTHES** (She survived.)

1912

MARCH Builders put the finishing touches on the *Titanic*.

APRIL 2 The *Titanic* completes its sea trials, then sails from Belfast, Northern Ireland, to Southampton, England.

APRIL 10 The *Titanic*'s maiden voyage begins in Southampton and ends in Cherbourg, France.

6

◄ **RUNNING A GIANT** machine like the *Titanic* required more than nine hundred workers. Among them were nine officers to supervise the crew, 390 stewards and stewardesses to serve the passengers' needs, and 289 firemen, trimmers, and greasers to carry and shovel coal into the boilers and lubricate moving parts of the ship. Seated at far left is Captain Smith.

FATAL FLAWS

The *TITANIC* could carry up to 3,547 people, yet it carried only 16 lifeboats and 4 collapsible boats with canvas sides—enough for just 1,178 people. At the time, British laws stated that the *TITANIC* had to carry only 16 lifeboats. By carrying the 4 collapsible boats, the *TITANIC* was actually carrying more than the law required.

"My pretty little cabin with its electric heater and pink curtains delighted me. Its beautiful lace quilt, and pink cushions, and photographs all round, it all looked so homey."
SURVIVOR LADY LUCILLE DUFF GORDON, FIRST-CLASS PASSENGER

WHITE STAR LINE
ROYAL & STEAMERS
UNITED STATES MAIL
SECOND CLASS ★ ★
TICKET PRICE: $65 ($1,159 in today's money)

▼ **THE *TITANIC'S*** second-class rooms were as good as first-class rooms on other ships. Most second-class passengers were professionals—teachers, doctors, and businessmen. Their rooms were simple but attractive, with mahogany beds and linoleum floors. Second-class passengers also had their own library and several other beautifully decorated public rooms (below).

FIRST-CLASS BEDROOM

GYMNASIUM

"Everything was new. New! Our cabin was just like a big hotel room, it was so big. The dining room was beautiful—the linens, all the bright polished silver you can imagine."
SURVIVOR RUTH BECKER, 12-YEAR-OLD SECOND-CLASS PASSENGER

WHITE STAR LINE
ROYAL & STEAMERS
UNITED STATES MAIL
THIRD CLASS ★
TICKET PRICE: $36 ($642 in today's money)

▼ **MOST THIRD-**class, or steerage, passengers were poor people leaving Europe for a new life in the U.S. Their accommodations on the lower decks were spare. However, the *Titanic* featured private cabins for two, four, or eight people, not 40, as was the case with many other transatlantic liners.

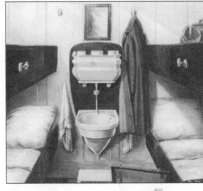

➤ **STEERAGE** passengers came from many different countries. (In fact, the ship carried people of 24 different nationalities.) During the early 1900s, immigration to the U.S. exploded, and shipping companies, like the White Star Line,

cashed in on it. On the average, a ticket on the *Titanic* cost steerage passengers two months' pay.

APRIL 11 The *Titanic* leaves Cherbourg on April 10 and arrives at Queenstown (now called Cobh), Ireland, around noon on the 11th to pick up the last of its passengers. Around 1:30 p.m., the *Titanic* departs for New York.

APRIL 13 The *Titanic* gets the first of seven ice warnings from other ships.

7

Disaster Strikes

The night that the *Titanic* sailed into history was cold and moonless. The normally storm-tossed Atlantic Ocean was a flat calm. That Sunday was cold, but it had been a pleasant one for the passengers. They had spent their time attending church services and relaxing. By 11 p.m., most of them were in bed.

First Officer William Murdoch was in charge on the bridge (the control center at the front of a ship) at 11:40 when the *Titanic*'s lookouts spotted the iceberg about 1,500 feet ahead. Murdoch reacted quickly, reversing the engines and ringing the warning bell, but less than 40 seconds later, the ship's starboard side scraped along the iceberg. From that moment on, the *Titanic* was doomed.

▼ **WHEN PEOPLE SAY,** "That's just the tip of the iceberg," they mean that it's part of something much bigger. That's because only about 10 percent of an iceberg is above water. The 90 percent below water may have sharp edges that could damage a ship's hull. Atlantic icebergs form when huge pieces of freshwater ice break off from glaciers and float into the sea.

TRY THIS!

THE ICEBERG punched a series of thin gashes along the first 250 feet of the *Titanic*, damaging six of the "watertight" compartments, which begin to flood. To get an idea of how this affected the rest of the ship, take an empty ice cube tray and slowly pour water into just one section. As it fills, notice how the water pours over the top into other sections.

➤ **THE *TITANIC* WAS** so big that most passengers and crew felt only a slight vibration when the ship hit the iceberg. Some also heard a noise, which one passenger described as the sound heavy cloth makes as it rips. Very few first- and second-class passengers were alarmed, even after they learned that the ship had hit an iceberg. After all, the *Titanic* was "unsinkable."

However, many steerage passengers, lower in the ship, realized the danger. The iceberg shown below was in the North Atlantic the night the *Titanic* sank.

FATAL FLAWS

During its journey, the TITANIC *received seven messages from other ships warning that icebergs were in the area. The telegraph operators delivered all messages to Captain Smith or the officers, except one, from the* MESABA. *Smith steered the ship farther south to avoid the icebergs, but he did not slow down. Like many captains at the time, he trusted his lookouts to spot trouble in time.*

"I jumped out of my bed, put on a pair of trousers, and ran up on the deck to find out what was the matter. I saw some small pieces of ice on the starboard side..."
SURVIVOR ERNEST ARCHER, SEAMAN

"I felt the engines slow and stop. The dancing motion and the vibrations ceased suddenly after being a part of our very existence for four days, and that was the first hint that anything out of the ordinary had happened. I jumped out of bed, I went out of my cabin into the hall. There was a steward leaning against the staircase. I said, 'Why have we stopped?' 'I don't know sir,' he replied, 'but I don't suppose it's anything much.'" **SURVIVOR LAWRENCE BEESLEY, SECOND-CLASS PASSENGER**

APRIL 14 — **11:40 p.m.** The *Titanic*, traveling at 21½ knots, collides with an iceberg.

11:50 p.m. Captain Smith and Thomas Andrews, the ship's designer, check for damage. Andrews informs the captain that the *Titanic* will sink because more than four bulkheads are damaged.

APRIL 15 — **Midnight** Captain Smith tells the ship's wireless operators to send a distress call.

8

SOS

As the *Titanic*'s forward compartments flooded, wireless operators Jack Phillips and Harold Bride frantically signaled other ships. At first, they sent the traditional Morse code distress call, CQD (Attention all stations: Distress). Several ships responded, but the nearest one, the *Carpathia*, was 58 miles, or more than four hours, away.

The radio operators then sent the newer SOS distress call, a signal that was easy to transmit and receive. In 1906, SOS (dot, dot, dot; dash, dash, dash; dot, dot, dot) had been created to replace the longer and more complicated CQD (dash, dot, dash, dot; dash, dash, dot, dash; dash, dot, dot).

Now, it was only a matter of time.

➤ **AT FIRST, THERE** was great confusion but no panic on board the sinking *Titanic*. On the port (left) side of the ship, the *Titanic*'s officers allowed only women and children into the lifeboats, as well as one or two crewmen to help row and steer. On the starboard (right) side, men could get into the lifeboats if no women or children were around to fill the spots. As the number of lifeboats dwindled, people became increasingly frightened.

▼ **SOME OF THE LIFE**-boat crews were so inept that the women took over. On Lifeboat No. 6, Denver millionaire

Molly Brown organized the women into rowing teams and helped keep spirits up. Known as a colorful, outspoken woman even before boarding the ship, the press later dubbed her "the unsinkable Molly Brown." A romanticized musical based on her life later became a hit play and movie.

"The escaping steam making a deafening noise, women and children were put into the boats first. When most of the boats had left the ship, she began to list forward. By this time, I had decided that the only thing to do was jump for my life. Having shaken hands with my two best friends, I climbed up on the boat deck railing and dropped about thirty feet into the sea."
SURVIVOR ALGERNON BARKWORTH, FIRST-CLASS PASSENGER

▲ **AMID THE DESPER**-ate search for lifeboat space, the ship's eight-man orchestra played lively tunes to help keep people calm. Meanwhile, below decks, engineers worked to keep the lights on. The boiler room crews had been dismissed to go topside. The generators were operating on leftover steam in the boilers, and as this subsided, the lights took on a reddish glow in the ship's final minutes. No musician or engineer survived.

> **CHECK IT OUT!**
> Did anyone predict the *Titanic*'s sinking?

FATAL FLAWS

The TITANIC had 20 lifeboats (including 4 collapsible ones) and davits (movable cranes for lowering the lifeboats into the water). The davits could hold a boat full of people, but the TITANIC's officers hadn't been told of this. As a result of one officer's fears of overloading, and because of people's unwillingness to leave loved ones, lifeboats that could have saved 1,178 people saved only 705.

2:05 a.m. Collapsible D is the last lifeboat launched. More than 1,500 people remain on the ship.

2:17 a.m. The *Titanic*'s last wireless message is sent. Captain Smith tells several people, "It's every man for himself."

2:18 a.m. The *Titanic* breaks in two pieces. The bow (front) section sinks. The stern (rear) section seems to stay afloat.

9

Endless Night

The only remains afloat of the *Titanic* after 2:20 a.m. were 20 lifeboats carrying just over seven hundred survivors. People in the boats were seasick and freezing. Nobody knew if or when a rescue ship would arrive.

For most of those swimming in the frigid water, there was little hope. One survivor said that their cries for help at first sounded like the crowd's roar at a baseball stadium when the batter hits a home run. But soon, the shouting faded away as the cold silenced the voices.

"Striking the water was like a thousand knives being driven into one's body." SURVIVOR CHARLES LIGHTOLLER, THE *TITANIC*'S SECOND OFFICER

➤ THE BIGGEST threat to people in the water was hypothermia, a dangerous lowering of the body's temperature. The salty seawater was around 28°F, four degrees below freezing, and no person could survive in it for more than a few minutes. Hypothermia causes the activity of the organs to slow down, and eventually they stop working.

▼ WHEN THE CARpathia got the message that the *Titanic* was in grave danger, it raced to help. In doing so, it had to ignore caution and run an obstacle course of icebergs in the dark. It took the *Carpathia* four hours to get everyone from the *Titanic*'s lifeboats on board. The ship's captain, Arthur Rostron (right), was awarded a specially commissioned Medal of Honor by the U.S. Congress.

TITANIC DISASTER GREAT LOSS OF LIFE EVENING NEWS

◄ SHIPS' RADIOS were all on the same frequency, causing messages from the *Titanic* and other ships to become garbled or merged. This left people on shore desperate for news. Some newspapers mistakenly reported that all the passengers had been saved. Others, lacking facts, made up stories. As the *Carpathia* entered New York harbor, crowds gathered, and people eagerly sought out loved ones.

S.S.TITANIC 5

10

CHECK IT OUT!

Can hypo-
thermia ever
save lives?

". . . and finally the ghastly noise
of the people thrashing about and
screaming and drowning, that
finally ceased. I remember saying
to my mother once, 'How dread-
ful that noise was,' and I always
remember her reply, and she
said, 'Yes, but think back about
the silence that followed it . . .' "
**SURVIVOR EVA HART, A SEVEN-YEAR-
OLD SECOND-CLASS PASSENGER**

FATAL FLAWS

*Despite the terrible cries for help, just one
lifeboat—No. 14 (below)—went back to pick up
people in the water. Those in the other boats
were afraid of being pulled down by the suc-
tion of the Titanic sinking (which, as it turned
out, was not very strong). They were also afraid
of being over-
turned by des-
perate people
trying to scram-
ble on board.
The lifeboat that
went back
found only four
people alive in
the water—and
one of them
soon died.*

◄ **FROM NEW YORK,** some survivors went to Washington, D.C., to testify about what had happened. Others went to Plymouth, England, aboard the *Lapland.* At Plymouth, they were taken to the train station (left) before going to testify at the British inquiry into the disaster.

3:30 a.m. Survivors in the lifeboats see signal rockets from the rescue ship, *Carpathia.*

4:10 a.m. Lifeboat No. 2 is the first picked up by the *Carpathia.*

8:30 a.m. Lifeboat No. 12 is the last one rescued. Three days later, the *Carpathia* arrives in New York with 705 *Titanic* survivors.

11

Titanic's Legacy

In the early 1900s, science and technology seemed to be making the world better all the time. New drugs eliminated diseases, and new inventions like the automobile made life easier. However, the sinking of the "unsinkable" *Titanic* rattled everyone's confidence in progress. The march of technology did not stop after April 15, 1912, but it did pause to learn a few lessons. The *Titanic* has remained a source of curiosity ever since.

CHINA SERVING PLATE

FIRST-CLASS DINNER PLATE

BANKNOTE

FIRST-CLASS DEMITASSE CUP

SILVERWARE

IN 1985, FRENCHMAN Jean-Louis Michel and American Robert Ballard led the team of scientists who discovered the wreck of the *Titanic*, two and a half miles below the surface of the Atlantic. Underwater cameras were lowered to explore the wreck. In 1986, Ballard returned to the site, this time with a submersible, *Alvin,* which for the first time enabled humans to visit the wreck.

▲ **FLORIDA-BASED** RMS Titanic, Inc. owns salvage rights to the *Titanic.* It has retrieved more than six thousand objects from the wreck. The company vowed not to sell objects with historical importance. However, with the approval of the British and French governments, it has sold lumps of coal from the ship to raise money. Some people protest the salvaging, saying that the *Titanic's* wreck is a gravesite. Others say the recovered objects themselves serve as a memorial to the *Titanic's* passengers and crew and provide valuable insights into life aboard the ship in 1912.

▼ **AT ONE TIME,** scientists studying the wreck believed that the iceberg did so much damage to the *Titanic* because the ship's steel had become brittle in cold water. However, newer research suggests that the steel was not likely to crack in cold temperatures. More likely, the steel bent or gave way due to the incredible force of the flooding water.

12

TITANIC SCAPEGOATS

◀ **ALMOST AS SOON** as the *Titanic*'s survivors reached New York, the press began looking for someone to blame. Survivor J. Bruce Ismay, managing director of the White Star Line, was their top target. The American press criticized him for boarding a lifeboat when so many others died.

▲ **WHILE THE *TITANIC*** was sinking, some on board saw the lights of a ship in the distance. The *Californian* was accused of being the mystery ship that left the *Titanic* to its fate. Later investigations found that this probably was not true: a third ship may have moved between them. Even so, the *Californian* may have seen the *Titanic*'s distress rockets. Also, the *Californian*'s radio operator had shut down its wireless for the night, as usual, so he never heard the *Titanic*'s calls for help.

> **CHECK IT OUT!**
>
> What happened to the *Titanic*'s sister ships, *Olympic* and *Gigantic?*

▼ **THE *TITANIC* HAS** inspired books, poems, plays, films, and songs. The first movie came out just one month after the ship sank and starred survivor Dorothy Gibson. Most people today know about the disaster through the 1997 hit movie *Titanic*, starring Leonardo DiCaprio and Kate Winslet.

▶ **TWO INVESTIGA-** tions into the sinking—one British, one American— led to big changes in how ships operated. Almost immediately, all ships had to carry enough lifeboats for all passengers, and lifeboat drills became mandatory. Every large ship also had to keep its wireless working at all times. Shipping lanes were shifted farther south to avoid icebergs, and an iceberg patrol was set up to chart and follow icebergs and issue warnings.

13

NAME _Mr. Henry Rogers_

WHITE STAR LINE

ROYAL AND UNITED STATES MAIL STEAMERS

ISMAY, IMRIE & CO.,
1 COCKSPUR STREET, S.W.,
38 LEADENHALL STREET, E.C.,
LONDON,
30 JAMES STREET
LIVERPOOL
AND
CANUTE ROAD, SOUTHAMPTON

Agent at PARIS –
NICHOLAS MARTIN, 9, Rue Scribe

WHITE STAR LINE
9 BROADWAY, NEW YORK,
84 STATE STREET, BOSTON

JAMES SCOTT & CO., Agents
QUEENSTOWN

NAME _Mr. Charles Frederick Waddington Sedgwick_

WHITE STAR LINE

ROYAL AND UNITED STATES MAIL STEAMERS

ISMAY, IMRIE & CO.,
1 COCKSPUR STREET, S.W.,
38 LEADENHALL STREET, E.C.,
LONDON,
30 JAMES STREET
LIVERPOOL
AND
CANUTE ROAD, SOUTHAMPTON

Agent at PARIS –
NICHOLAS MARTIN, 9, Rue Scribe

WHITE STAR LINE
9 BROADWAY, NEW YORK,
84 STATE STREET, BOSTON

JAMES SCOTT & CO., Agents
QUEENSTOWN

TITANIC
Past and Present

by Edward S. Kamuda

Additional text and editing by Karen Kamuda, Paul Louden-Brown

While passengers and crew were having lunch, wireless operators, John George "Jack" Phillips and Harold Bride, were busy catching up on a backlog of passenger messages. The previous evening the wireless set had broken down and not until early Sunday morning were the two men able to send or receive messages. Wireless telegraphy was fairly new, and many ships had none. Bride and Phillips worked for the Marconi Company who installed the sets on ships as a franchise, encouraging people to use the new technology to send messages back to land. Operators were paid per message. Until the miracle of wireless telegraphy, when a ship was at sea for weeks there was virtually no communication until she landed.

At 1:40 pm the operators' working routine was disturbed by an incoming message from the White Star liner Baltic: "Captain Smith, Titanic. Have had moderate variable winds and clear fine weather since leaving. Greek steamer Athinai reports passing icebergs and large quantities of field ice today in latitude 41.51 N. longitude 49.11 W...Wish you and Titanic all success. Commander." This particular message was handed directly to Captain Smith, who, instead of posting it in the chart room, gave it to Bruce Ismay who casually put it in his pocket. Later in the day Smith asked for it back. Smith was very

aware of the danger from ice. On Friday he had received ice warnings from the French Line vessel La Touraine and on Saturday Furness, Withy & Company's steamer Rappahannock reported having passed through heavy field ice.

Titanic steamed on and had passed this area without spotting any ice but messages from Baltic and the Cunard liner Caronia indicated that ice would continue to pose a threat during the voyage. Smith altered course steaming sixteen miles further south before making the turn, at the so-called "corner" and headed due west towards the Nantucket Lightship.

From the German steamer Amerika wireless operator Otto Reuter sent at 1:45 PM: "Amerika passed two large icebergs in 41 degrees 27' N., 50 degrees 8' W., on the 14th April."

Previous messages had been promptly delivered to the bridge but this one never got there. Titanic's wireless unexpectedly went dead and Phillips, busy trouble shooting, shoved aside probably the most critical ice warning. (This important document is in the Titanic Museum, Titanic Historical Society collection). By early evening, Phillips finally got the set operating.

Approaching the iceberg danger zone, Titanic remained on course, her powerful quadruple-expansion engines and single low pressure turbine drove the liner smoothly through the water at a moderate 22.5 knots. The temperature was falling fast and by 8:55 PM it was only one degree above freezing. Second Officer Charles Lightoller sent word to the ship's carpenter John Hutchinson to see that the fresh water supply did not freeze. Soon afterwards Captain Smith entered the bridge and together with Lightoller discussed the conditions.

They noted the lack of wind and the unruffled sea. Up in the crow's nest lookouts Frederick Fleet and Reginald Lee had been told to keep a "sharp eye peeled" for small ice and growlers.

The night was crystal clear; there was no moon and the sky was filled with stars. The sea looked as smooth as plate glass, paradoxically, a disadvantage for the lookouts. Without waves breaking around an iceberg's base leaving a wake, it would be hard to spot without reflective moonlight, especially if a berg was showing its dark side.

Having assured himself that all was well, Captain Smith retired for the night, with the instruction "If in the slightest degree doubtful, let me know." Lightoller continued to peer into the darkness. Out beyond the ship's bow lay an inky, black expanse of water.

Phillips, the senior operator was interrupted by a message from the Atlantic Transport Line steamer Mesaba. The message read: "Ice report. In latitude 42 north to 41.25 north, longitude 49 west to longitude 50.3 west. Saw much heavy pack ice and great number large icebergs, also field ice. Weather good, clear."

Phillips replied: "Received, thanks." Mesaba's wireless operator waited to hear that the message had been relayed to the captain and sent two words: "Stand by." Instead Phillips continued sending the backlog of passenger messages to Cape Race. Another ice warning that was never delivered to the bridge.

At ten o'clock, First Officer William Murdoch

relieved Lightoller. The two men chatted briefly about the falling temperature, now down to 32 degrees and the emphatic reminder to the lookouts to be on their toes for any signs of icebergs. Lightoller then went below leaving Murdoch to the darkness and freezing night air.

By 11:30 PM most passengers had gone to bed, but a few night owls were gathered around a card table in the first class smoking room. In the main dining saloon, stewards preparing for Monday morning breakfast, carefully arranged gleaming silverplate and fine china edged in 22k gold on immaculate damask linen. As her passengers slept or relaxed, Titanic in a blaze of light from her sidelights illuminating the ambient darkness, forged steadily ahead, speed unabated, a white wave of foam curling around her bow. The clock on the first class grand staircase decorated with a carved panel of two classical figures representing Honor and Glory crowning Time showed 11:40 PM

A few moments later Fleet in the crow's nest began to make out what was at first, a small, irregular black object directly in their path. "There is ice ahead" he said to Lee, the other lookout, as he instinctively rang the crow's nest bell three times indicating to the bridge that something lay directly ahead.

Sixth Officer James Moody answered the telephone; "What did you see?" "Iceberg, right ahead!" shouted Fleet. Without emotion in his voice Moody said "Thank you." replaced the receiver and called loudly to Murdoch "Iceberg, right ahead." By now the First Officer had already seen the iceberg and rushed to the engine room telegraph moving the handles to "Stop" then "Full Speed Astern" and immediately ordered "hard a starboard." Moody standing behind the helmsman, Quartermaster Robert Hitchens, replied, "hard a starboard. The helm is hard over, sir."

The 46,000-ton liner seemed to take a prolonged length of time, gradually responding to her helm and began to turn to port. Murdoch intended to order "hard a port" to bring the stern away from the iceberg but it was too late; she struck. And as the iceberg glided by, breaking iron rivet heads fastening the steel shell plates causing massive leakage below the waterline, tons of ice fell onto the fo'c'sle and well deck. Murdoch closed the electric switch controlling the watertight doors. Deep inside the ship's alarm bells rang as the massive watertight doors sealed each of the liner's sixteen compartments.

Walter Belford was Titanic's night chief baker. "We were working on the fifth deck amidships baking for the next day. There was a shudder all through the ship about 11:40 PM The provisions came tumbling down and the oven doors came open.

Captain Smith rushed onto the bridge; "What have we struck?" he asked. "An iceberg, sir," replied Murdoch. Then the First Officer explained what he had done.

After receiving an initial report that no damage was found, Smith ordered the carpenter to go down and "sound" the ship. When he returned he had bad news that Titanic was taking on water. Soon passengers began noticing the lack of vibration from the engines and worried about the impact from the collision.

J. Bruce Ismay, in his suite on B-deck, was awakened by scraping noises. He quickly put on an coat over his pajamas, made his way to the bridge and asked Smith "Do you think the ship is seriously damaged?" Smith replied, "I am afraid she is."

Thomas Andrews had gone below and gave his assessment of the damage to Smith. In less than 10 seconds Titanic's first six watertight compartments had been opened to the sea by the iceberg. The first five; the forepeak, number 1, 2, 3 holds and number 6 boiler room were flooding uncontrollably. The flooding in boiler room number 5 was controlled by the engine room pumps, but the sheer weight of water, in the first five compartments, drew the liner's bow down, pulling her head lower and lower. A critical design flaw her watertight compartments which did not reach high enough, allowed water to flow from one compartment into another like liquid flowing in an ice cube tray. That Titanic would founder was a mathematical certainty. The only question was when? Andrews estimated another hour. The recent theory put forward that Titanic sank principally due to poor grade steel or brittle steel is not only untrue, it is also a moot point.

At first there was an understandable reluctance from some passengers in first and second class when stewards ordered them to put on their lifejackets and go up on deck. To leave the warmth and safety of their stateroom at midnight when all was quiet and nothing seemingly alarming happening didn't make sense. In third class it was a different story, a complicating factor was United States Immigration regulations which required gates on immigrant ships (Titanic was officially listed as an Emigrant Ship) to separate steerage (third class). Stewards had difficulty with language and perhaps fearing a stampede for the lifeboats, some stewards kept passengers below until they received word for them to be allowed on deck.

©2001-2004 The Titanic Historical Society, Inc

www.titanichistoricalsociety.org & www.titanic1.org

THE OFFICIAL WEBSITE OF THE TITANIC HISTORICAL SOCIETY, INC.

MOON

Moon remembers.

Marooned in shadowed night,

white powder plastered

on her pockmarked face,

scarred with craters,

filled with waterless seas,

she thinks back

to the Eagle,

to the flight

of men from Earth,

of rocks sent back in space,

and one

faint

footprint

in the Sea of Tranquility.

SECRETS

Space keeps its secrets
                 hidden

It does not tell.

                 Are black holes time machines?
                 Where do lost comets go?

        Is Pluto moon or planet?

How many, how vast
        unknown galaxies beyond us?

        Do other creatures
        dwell   on distant spheres?

                        Will we ever know?

Space is silent.

It seldom answers.

        But we ask.

HOUSES

In ancient times, the Maya lived in the mountains and rain forests. Imagine trying to build a home on a mountain or in a rain forest. Most of the ancient Maya lived in simple homes. They made their homes from materials that were nearby, such as vines, mud, and wood. Farmers lived in huts near their fields. A hut usually had one or two rooms. It had a dirt floor. The roof was made out of long grass or the leaves of palm trees.

Rulers sat on "thinking" mats.

Rich families lived near the town centers. They had large houses with many rooms. The rooms were divided by cotton cloths. The walls were made out of stone and covered with stucco, a kind of plaster. These homes usually had a **patio** at their center. Family members ate and relaxed there. Statues of the gods stood outside these homes to protect them.

Today, many Maya people live in small houses in the country. The homes are much like those of the ancient Maya. Inside the homes are mats. The mats are where everyone sits. Long ago, mats were used as "thinking" chairs. People sat on the mats to think. Today, the Maya still use their mats as a place to think.

This thatched-roof house looks like a Maya house of long ago.

8

CLOTHES

In ancient times, how did the Maya stay cool in their tropical climate? They grew cotton, wove it into cloth, and made it into clothes. Their clothes were usually white. White cotton clothes were cool in the heat. Sometimes, they used plant dyes to add color or designs to cloth.

LOOKING BACK

The ancient Maya thought that flat heads were a sign of beauty. When their children were born, they placed the baby's head between two boards. This would flatten and lengthen the head. The Maya also thought crossed eyes were a sign of beauty. They hung a colorful bead between a baby's eyes to encourage crossed eyes!

©H.M. Herget/NGS Image Collection

To stay cool, men usually wore just loincloths. Women wore skirts and long shirts or loose dresses. People went either barefoot or they wore sandals made of straw or leather.

The ancient Maya liked tattoos. They loved jewelry, too. Men wore huge earrings, necklaces, and bracelets. Men wore more jewelry than women. Rich people also wore large **headdresses**, sometimes decorated with colorful feathers.

Today, most Maya wear the same kinds of clothes that are popular in the United States. Some women still handweave white cloth for shawls, men's shirts, and children's clothes. Women also embroider bright designs using ancient patterns.

9

How do we solve the growing power problem? Why not just build more power plants? After all, that's worked in the past. So why not? Well, power plants are expensive. Also, how many people want a power plant in their backyards?

But there is an even bigger problem—the environment. Today almost two-thirds of the electrical power we use comes from power plants that use **fossil fuels** to make electricity. Fossil fuels, such as oil, coal, and natural gas, are burned to make electricity. Burning fossil fuels releases pollution and carbon dioxide gas into the air. As more carbon dioxide is released into the air, more heat gets trapped near Earth's surface. The more fossil fuels we burn, the warmer the air around Earth gets. So building fossil fuel plants is not always the best answer.

Blow, Wind, Blow

Luckily, burning fossil fuels isn't the only way to make electricity. For example, people have been using the power of wind for centuries. So why can't we use this energy to make electricity? Well, we can. In very windy places, power companies have installed dozens—even hundreds—of large windmills. Windmills change the energy of moving air into clean electrical power. Wind power won't solve all our energy problems, but it can help meet some of the demand in certain places.

Power plants that burn fossil fuels can release pollution and large amounts of carbon dioxide into the air.

©Hugh Rose/Visuals Unlimited

23

Here Comes the Sun

If you're looking for a source of energy that doesn't pollute, look to the sun. The sun provides most of the heat and light on our planet. Since the late 1800s, scientists have been working to turn the sun's energy into electricity using devices called **solar cells**. The problem is, solar cells are expensive. But scientists are hopeful that someday soon, everybody will be able to take advantage of the sun's energy to make electricity.

Energy From Atoms

There are other ways to make electricity without burning fossil fuels. Scientists have learned how to change some types of atoms into other types of atoms. When this happens a large amount of energy is given off. This energy from atoms, called **nuclear energy**, has been used to make electricity for more than 50 years. Today about 10 percent of all the electricity used in the United States comes from this source. So why don't we build more nuclear power plants?

Although nuclear power doesn't pollute the air like the burning of fossil fuels does, there is a major drawback. The waste products from nuclear power plants are dangerous and must be stored in safe places. Many people are concerned about the safety of nuclear power.

Solar cells on the side of a house

©Superstock, Inc.

24

At Home in the Arctic

A huge polar bear lies sprawled on the smooth sea ice, white on white. Only its black nose and eyes stand out. Blustery winds begin to ruffle its thick, shaggy fur. Ah, home, freezing home!

Polar bears thrive in all polar regions of the Northern Hemisphere, including Russia, Norway, Greenland, Canada, and Alaska. While you and most other animals might find living in the Arctic hard to "bear," these amazing mammals have many **adaptations,** or features, that help them live quite comfortably in a frozen **habitat.**

Warm Coats

Their fur is an excellent natural coat. It is actually two layers. The inside layer is a woolly band of short hairs that provides **insulation,** or protection, against the cold. The outer layer is made up of long, clear hairs that reflect light and make polar bears appear white. White, of course, serves as **camouflage,** or a disguise, while hunting for **prey** in the snow.

Under all that fur, the skin is actually black. This helps absorb the sun's rays and keep the bears warm in temperatures as low as 50° below zero.

12

PHOTO/NORBERT ROSING

Built-in Snowshoes

Polar bears' broad paws (which are about 12 inches wide!) help them to walk on ice and packed snow. The paws work the way snowshoes would, by spreading out the bears' great weight. (Females can weigh around 600 pounds, and males can weigh up to 1,600 pounds. That's more than nine adult people put together!)

The soles of the polar bears' feet are covered with soft, small bumps and long hairs to create friction and make it easier to walk on slippery patches of ice.

Swim Gear

Polar bears are such super swimmers that their scientific name is *Ursus maritimus,* or "sea bear." They spend a lot of time in water, searching for food or swimming from place to place. Those large paws act like paddles in the water. A sleek shape, slick fur, and short tail and ears also make their bodies well suited for swimming. Their nostrils close up under water, and a thin, clear layer of tissue over their eyes acts just like goggles—it lets the bears keep their eyes open under water. Polar bears can swim more than six miles an hour for 10 straight hours.

13

Natural Hunting Tools

Polar bears are the largest **carnivores,** or animal eaters, on land. Their favorite food is baby ring seals. Polar bears have extremely sensitive noses and can smell a seal more than 20 miles away! Their powerful eyes can see one about 15 miles away. To catch a seal meal, a bear lies quietly at the edge of a hole in the ice and waits until a seal comes up for air. The bear then quickly grabs the seal and kills it with its sharp teeth.

From Season to Season

Most of the year, polar bears roam and hunt by themselves. But like many other animals, they do special things during certain seasons.

Spring. In early spring, males and females find each other, fatten up on seals, and mate. Feasting on seals lets polar bears add a thick layer of **blubber** for the rest of the year. Their bodies can live off this blubber when the seasons change and it becomes harder to find food. This four-inch layer of fat also keeps them warm.

Summer. When Arctic ice melts in summer, polar bears move inland and eat whatever they can find—rodents, eggs, berries, seaweed, or animals killed and left by other predators.

Fall. In October or November, pregnant females build **dens,** or caves, in the snowbanks and **hibernate** there through the winter. When polar bears hibernate, their heart rates slow down, and their body temperatures fall slightly, so they use less energy and can live off their stored blubber. Males and non-pregnant females

△ **In the Swim.** Polar bears are super swimmers.

◁ **On the Prowl.** Big paws and long claws are "handy" tools for catching baby seals.

PHOTOS/FLIP NICKLIN-MINDEN PICTURES

do not hibernate. They are on the move all through the winter, building temporary shelters only during big storms.

Winter. Females have their babies, or **cubs,** in December or January. They usually have twins. The cubs weigh only one pound when they are born and are only about a foot long. But they grow quickly from feeding on their mother's milk.

By the time the mother leaves her den in late March or early April, the cubs weigh 30 pounds. This is also exactly the time when baby seals are born, and the mother can begin to hunt. Cubs stay with their mother for about two years,

The Bear Facts

Weight: Male, 800–1,600 pounds; Female, 500–600 pounds

Length: Up to 10 feet

Favorite Food: Baby ring seals

Life Span: 15–18 years in the wild; 30–35 years in captivity

Home: Arctic shores, ice, and waters

Litter Size: 1–3

Enemies: Human hunters

COLD QUESTIONS

1 How have other Arctic animals adapted to the cold?

2 What type of adaptations would you need to survive in an Arctic habitat?

3 What do you think polar bears will do if there is less polar ice in the future?

14

learning how to hunt, hide, and survive in their cold habitat.

Less Ice Time?

For many years, humans widely hunted polar bears for their fur. During that time, bear populations began to drop greatly. Then in the 1970s, all countries with polar bears passed laws to protect them from being overhunted. Today, there are about 20,000 polar bears in the world.

Now scientists worry that polar bears may be facing a new problem that is caused by **global warming.** Global warming is the gradual rising temperature of Earth due to the additional release of carbon dioxide by human activities.

Recently some scientists noticed that global warming was causing Arctic ice to melt earlier in the spring and form later in the fall. Because polar bears depend on ice to find seals, less ice time means they may not get enough to eat.

Energy burned to run cars, trucks, homes, and factories can produce a lot of carbon dioxide. You and your family can help slow global warming by using less of this energy. For example:

■ Ride a bike instead of taking a car.
■ Encourage your friends to carpool.
■ Turn off lights when you're not using them.

Your energy-saving actions could help polar bears thrive in the Arctic for years to come!

Sea Hunt.
Polar bears spend a lot of time hunting baby seals on ice packs that float in the Arctic Ocean.

PHOTO/JAMES BRANDENBURG/MINDEN PICTURES

WebLink

Polar Bear Hotline
Check out www.polarbearsalive.org, the website of an organization dedicated to protecting polar bears.

Wordwise

adaptation: any feature that helps a living thing survive in its environment

blubber: a thick layer of fat under the skin

camouflage: a color or pattern that helps an animal hide in its environment

carnivore: an animal that eats another animal

cub: a young carnivore, such as a bear or fox

den: a place for resting or hiding

global warming: the rising temperature of the Earth due to increased carbon dioxide in the air

habitat: the place where something lives

hibernate: to spend the winter in a sleeplike state

insulation: something that prevents heat from passing through

prey: an animal that is hunted for food

15

14 One If by Land, Two If by Sea

An American rifle-man, better equipped than most of his fellow revolutionaries.

Three men rode horseback on an April night in 1775: Paul Revere, William Dawes, and Dr. Samuel Prescott. Each carried the same message: "The redcoats are coming." You may have heard of Paul Revere, because a poet, Henry Wadsworth Longfellow, wrote a famous poem about his ride.

Listen, my children, and you shall hear
Of the midnight ride of Paul Revere,
On the eighteenth of April, in Seventy-five;
Hardly a man is now alive
Who remembers that famous day and year.

Can you hear Longfellow making his words gallop, like a horse's hoofs? Here's more of the story, this time in prose:

The Patriots were worried. It looked as if war with Britain couldn't be avoided. The Patriots were the colonists who wanted independence. They wanted to be free of British rule. The other colonists—the ones who wanted to stay British subjects—were called Loyalists. Some Patriots, like Samuel Adams, expected war. But most Patriots still hoped to find peaceful ways to settle their differences with England.

It was scary to think of war. England was a great power; the colonies were scattered and had little military experience.

Still, it made sense to be prepared for the worst, so New Englanders began to stockpile cannonballs and gunpowder. They piled them up in Concord, a small town about 20 miles northwest of Boston.

When the British officers heard about those munitions, they decided to get them. Paul Revere and his Boston friends learned of the

On September 11, 1774, Dr. Joseph Warren and a group of Patriots gathered in Milton, Massachusetts, where they wrote out 19 blunt statements (called "resolves") protesting Britain's actions in the Boston area. Paul Revere carried those resolves to the Continental Congress in Philadelphia, where they are said to have influenced the delegates and a declaration they were writing.

Pamphlet: *An American Time Capsule* Library of Congress, Rare Book and Special Collections Division.

Advertisements like this one, for volunteers to fight for the colonies, were soon plastered around Boston.

69

Map: "The Shot Heard Round The World"
© 1993, 1999, 2003 by Wendy Frost and
Elspeth Leacock.

British plans. They found out that the redcoats were going to march on Concord the next morning!

Besides the gunpowder, Revere was worried about his friends Sam Adams and John Hancock. They were hiding in Lexington, right next door to Concord. The British were searching for those two troublemakers—they wanted to hang them as traitors.

Someone had to get a warning to those towns—and fast. It would help to know which way the redcoats would march.

Who Started It?

The story of Lexington and Concord as seen in Massachusetts and in England:

The troops came in sight just before sunrise...the Commanding Officer accosted the militia in words to this effect: "Disperse, you rebels, damn you, throw down your arms and disperse," upon which the [American] troops huzzaed, and immediately one or two [British] officers discharged their pistols, which were instantaneously followed by the firing of four or five of the soldiers, and then there seemed to be a general discharge from the whole body. Eight of our men were killed and nine wounded.

—FROM THE *SALEM GAZETTE*,
SALEM, MASSACHUSETTS, APRIL 25, 1775

Six companies of light infantry...at Lexington found a body of the country people under arms, on a green close to the road. And upon the King's troops marching up to them, in order to inquire the reason of their being so assembled, they went off in great confusion. And several guns were fired upon the King's troops from behind a stone wall, and also from the meeting house and other houses.... In consequence of this attack by the rebels, the troops returned the fire and killed several of them.

—FROM THE *LONDON GAZETTE*,
LONDON, ENGLAND, JUNE 10, 1775

A *green* is a grassy lawn or common. Many New England villages have a green for public gatherings. To *accost* someone means to approach and speak to or touch him or her—but not gently.

Disperse means to break up and scatter.
Huzza is an old-fashioned word for "yell." It's something like "hurrah." The rebels were yelling at the British soldiers.

From A History of US: From Colonies to Country (Vol. 3) by Joy Hakim, ©1993 by Joy Hakim.
Used by permission of Oxford University Press, Inc.

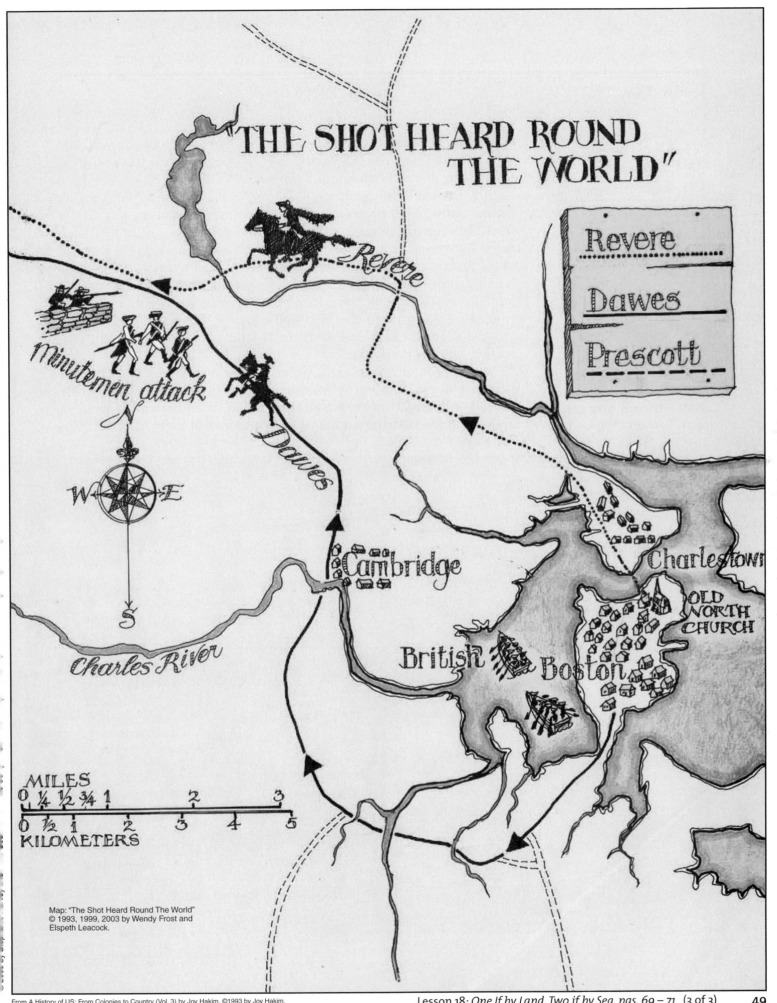

"THE SHOT HEARD ROUND THE WORLD"

Revere

Dawes

Prescott

Minutemen attack

N
W E
S

Charles River

Cambridge

Charlestown

OLD NORTH CHURCH

British Boston

MILES
0 ¼ ½ ¾ 1   2   3

0 ½ 1   2   3   4   5
KILOMETERS

Map: "The Shot Heard Round The World"
© 1993, 1999, 2003 by Wendy Frost and
Elspeth Leacock.

Grenadiers, dragoons, regulars, redcoats—they're all British soldiers.

Redcoats march through Concord looking for weapons and ammunition while their officers spy out the land. **Too late.**

Would they go by the long land route over the Boston neck? Or would they take the shorter route—by boat across the water to Charlestown and then on foot from there?

Billy Dawes didn't wait to find out. He pretended to be a drunk farmer and staggered past the British sentry who stood guard at the neck. As soon as he was out of sight of the guard, Dawes jumped on a horse and went at a gallop. He knew the redcoats would start out soon, and he shouted that message at each Patriot house he passed.

That same dark night Paul Revere sent someone to spy on the British. "Find out which way the redcoats will march," the spy was told. "Then climb into the high bell tower of the North Church and send a signal. Light one lantern if they go by land. Hang two lanterns if they go by sea."

Revere got in a boat and quietly rowed out into the Charles River. A horse was ready for him on the Charlestown shore. He waited—silently. (Revere was a known Patriot and would have been arrested if the British had found him outdoors at night.)

"A View of the Town of Concord" by Amos Doolittle.
The Connecticut Historical Society, Hartford, Connecticut.

And lo! as he looks, on the belfry's height
A glimmer, and then a gleam of light!
He springs to the saddle, the bridle he turns,
But lingers and gazes, till full on his sight
A second lamp in the belfry burns!

Now he knew! The redcoats would take the water route across the Charles River, just as Paul Revere was doing. What happened next? Well, both Billy Dawes and Paul Revere rode hard, through the night, warning everyone in the countryside that the British were coming. They met at Lexington in time to tell Sam Adams and John Hancock to escape. But before they could go on to Concord, they were stopped by a British patrol. The redcoats took their horses. Luckily, by this time, a third man, Dr. Samuel Prescott, was riding with Dawes and Revere. (Prescott had been visiting the girl he intended to marry, who lived in Lexington.) The doctor managed to escape from the British, ride home to Concord, and warn everyone there.

The American farmers were ready, and they grabbed their guns. They were called "minutemen" because they could fight on a minute's notice. (Some had been trained fighting in the French and Indian War.) Captain John Parker was the leader of the minutemen, and what he said on that day is now carved in stone near the spot where he must have stood. "Stand your ground. Don't fire unless fired upon. But if they mean to have a war let it begin here!"

And it did begin right there, at Lexington. Each side said the other fired the first shot. No one knows who really did, but a poet named Ralph Waldo Emerson called it "the shot heard round the world." (Can you see why?)

When the smoke cleared, eight American farmers lay dead. It was April 19, 1775. The American Revolution had begun.

But it was gunpowder that the redcoats had set out to get, so they marched on—to Concord—but they couldn't find the powder. That made them so angry they started a fire. "Will you let them burn the town down?" shouted one colonist. "No, I haven't a man who is afraid

The stanza with Ralph Waldo Emerson's famous line goes like this:

By the rude bridge that
   arched the flood,
Their flag to April's breeze
   unfurled,
Here once the embattled
   farmers stood,
And fired the shot heard
   round the world.

Senior Citizen's Arrest

One of the best stories of the Revolutionary War involves an old woman. She was called Mother Batherick, and she lived near Concord. On the day of the famous battle, all the young men of her town became minutemen and rushed off to fight, leaving behind a group of old men. They were supposed to guard the town. The old soldiers chose as their leader a veteran of the French and Indian War, a black man whose name was David Lamson. Lamson and his men were all behind a stone wall when some British supply wagons came by. Lamson told the redcoats to halt. They didn't, and the old warriors fired. Two British soldiers and four horses went down. The other redcoats ran.

Mother Batherick was digging weeds at a nearby pond. Six breathless British soldiers rushed up and surrendered to her. She turned them over to Lamson and his old troopers. After that, Americans liked to ask this question: "If one old lady can capture six grenadiers, how many soldiers will King George need to conquer America?"

73

"Paul Revere" by John Singleton Copley
Museum of Fine Arts, Boston

Paul Revere in his regular job as a silversmith, showing off one of his teapots. This portrait was painted by John Singleton Copley, a leading colonial artist.

to go," said the minutemen's Captain Isaac Davis. The British stood at the North Bridge in Concord. They fired at the colonists. The minutemen fired back. Now the British were scared, and they tried to retreat. The Americans followed and whipped the redcoats. More than two Englishmen fell for every American casualty.

Do you know the song "Yankee Doodle"? Well, the British made it up to insult the Americans. They said a Yankee Doodle was a backwoods hick who didn't know how to fight. When the British marched to Concord and Lexington, they wore their fancy red uniforms, and their drummers and pipers played "Yankee Doodle."

After the battle, it was the Americans who sang that song. They said, "We'll be Yankee Doodles and proud of it!"

But that isn't the whole story. There is always more to war than winning or losing. These are words written in 1775:

Isaac Davis...was my husband. He was then thirty years of age. We had four children; the youngest about fifteen months old....The alarm was given early in the morning, and my husband lost no time in making ready to go to Concord with his company...[he] said but little that morning. He seemed serious and thoughtful; but never seemed to hesitate....He only said, "Take good care of the children." In the afternoon he was brought home a corpse.

Yankee Doodle

Yankee Doodle went to town,
  A-ridin' on a pony.
Stuck a feather in his cap
And called it Macaroni.

Chorus:
Yankee Doodle, keep it up,
Yankee Doodle Dandy,
Mind the music and the step
And with the girls be handy.

Father and I went down to camp,
Along with Captain Gooding,
And there we saw the men and boys
As thick as hasty pudding.

(Chorus)
And there we saw a thousand men,
As rich as Squire David;

And what they wasted every day,
I wish it could be savèd.

(Chorus)
And there was Captain Washington
Upon a slapping stallion,
A-giving orders to his men;
I guess there was a million.

(Chorus)
And there I saw a little keg,
Its head was made of leather;
They knocked upon it with two sticks
To call the men together.

(Chorus)
And there I saw a swamping gun,
As big as a log of maple,

Upon a mighty little cart,
A load for father's cattle.

(Chorus)
And every time they fired it off
It took a horn of powder,
It made a noise like father's gun,
Only a nation louder.

(Chorus)
I can't tell you half I saw,
They kept up such a smother,
So I took my hat off, made a bow
And scampered home to mother.

(to tune of chorus)
Yankee Doodle is the tune
Americans delight in.
'Twill do to whistle, sing or play
And just the thing for fightin'.

74

After Lexington and Con-
cord, a known British
sympathizer—a Loyalist—
could be strung up and
ridiculed, like this man,
or sometimes find a worse
fate.

Henry Wadsworth Longfellow finished the story:

*You know the rest. In the books you have read
How the British Regulars fired and fled,—
How the farmers gave them ball for ball,
From behind each fence and farmyard wall,
Chasing the redcoats down the lane,
Then crossing the fields to emerge again
Under the trees at the turn of the road,
And only pausing to fire and load.*

*So through the night rode Paul Revere;
And so through the night went his cry of alarm
To every Middlesex village and farm,—
A cry of defiance and not of fear,
A voice in the darkness, a knock at the door,
And a word that shall echo forevermore!
For, borne on the night-wind of the Past,
Through all our history, to the last,
In the hour of darkness and peril and need,
The people will waken and listen to hear
The hurrying hoof-beats of that steed,
And the midnight message of Paul Revere.*

The people of New England
did not wish for war. This
was not a warrior culture...
and showed none of the
martial spirit that has appeared in so many other
times and places. There
were no cheers or celebrations when the militia de-
parted....The people of New
England knew better than
that. In 140 years they had
gone to war at least once in
every generation, and
some of those conflicts had
been cruel and bloody.
Many of the men who mus-
tered that morning were
themselves veterans of
savage fights against the
French and Indians. They
and their families knew
what war could do.
—*DAVID HACKETT FISCHER,
PAUL REVERE'S RIDE*

CAN KIDS STOP KIDS FROM SMOKING?

Not for Sale! Not for Sale!" About 700 teen-agers shouted those words at a gathering in New Jersey last week. The teens belong to a group called REBEL (Reaching Everyone by Exposing Lies). They were sending a message to cigarette companies.

"The way cigarette makers target kids with ads makes me sick," said REBEL's Jessie Smolin, 17. "We're not for sale. They can't buy us."

Each year 400,000 Americans die of

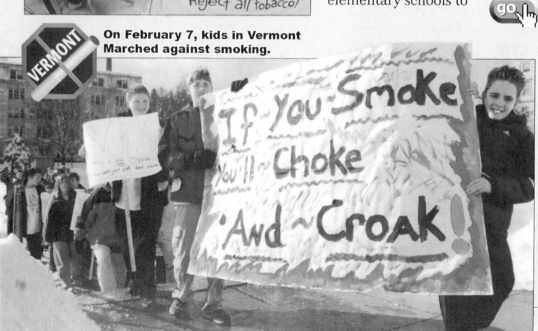

Kids work on Frontline Projects.

you Better tell Somebody!

R.A.T.

Reject all tobacco!

diseases caused by smoking. Studies show that the earlier kids try smoking, the greater their chances of becoming addicted and dying of smoking-related illnesses.

Kids Fight Back

To stop kids from getting started, many states are getting kids to help. In Mississippi, high school students belonging to a group called Frontline visit elementary schools to

teach kids why they shouldn't smoke. Last year the group helped pass a law that forbids smoking at school sports events. Since the program began two years ago, teen smoking in Mississippi has dropped.

The same thing happened in Florida after a group called Truth involved kids in creating antismoking ads. The very successful ads now run on national TV.

Surprisingly, money for these programs comes from tobacco companies. In 1998 the companies agreed to pay $250 billion to 46 states for harming people's health. A few states are using some of that money to pay for antismoking programs created by kids.

"Tobacco companies try to tell kids it's cool to smoke," says Leonardo Casas, 16, of REBEL. "We frame the message so that kids can see it's cooler not to."

—By Ritu Upadhyay

 For more on smoking, click *www.timeforkids.com/smoke*

On February 7, kids in Vermont Marched against smoking.

If You Smoke You'll Choke And Croak!

What if cigarette ads told the TRUTH?

 The Truth campaign began in Florida. Now its ads run nationwide.

TIME FOR KIDS

Western Roundup

More than 45,000 wild horses run free in the American West. The horses have roamed this land for centuries. Now these wild herds are running out of food and space. For the past 29 years, the U.S. government has tried to keep the herds under control by rounding up some of the horses and putting them up for adoption. Not everyone agrees with the government's actions.

Home on the Range?

Some animal rights groups think the horses should run free. They have gone to court to fight a plan to remove more horses from the wild.

But government officials say the horse population has grown out of control. One reason is that horses no longer have many natural predators such as wolves. Many horses are starving because there isn't enough food for a huge herd. Also, ranchers need open areas to graze cattle. They say that the horses compete with cattle for food and water.

The courts will decide the future of these wild beasts. But some people are already trying to help. Dayton O. Hyde is a wild horse lover and a rancher. In 1988, he decided to use his own money to set up a safe place for wild horses. Now about 400 wild horses live on his land. He hopes others will follow his example. Says Hyde: "The horses are happy here."   —*Kathryn R. Hoffman*

Government wranglers catch a wild horse in Nevada last month.

MONICA ALMEIDA—THE NEW YORK TIMES

JEFF VANUGA—CORBIS

go Round up more facts at *timeforkids.com/horses*

MONICA ALMEIDA—THE NEW YORK TIMES

These horses may be adopted and tamed.

Western States with Wild Horses

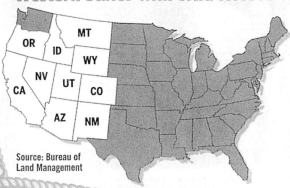

OR | ID | MT | WY
NV | UT | CO
CA | AZ | NM

Source: Bureau of Land Management

WHAT'S THE SCOOP?

What factors affect the size of the horse population? What would happen if the horses were left alone?

Turn It Off!

STEVE SMITH—GETTY IMAGES

On April 22, millions of televisions around the world will go blank. Then, TV viewers everywhere will take drastic action. Entire families and groups of friends will head outdoors to ride bikes or to play. Will you join in—or will you just sit there and watch?

April 22-28 is TV-Turnoff Week. A group called TV-Turnoff

Network started the yearly event in 1995. This year, people in every U.S. state and more than 12 countries are expected to take part.

Too Much TV

Each year, kids in the U.S. spend more time glued to the tube than doing anything else—except for sleeping. Many health care groups are concerned. Studies show that watching too much TV, with its violent shows and ads for junk food, may lead to bad eating habits, too little exercise and bad behavior.

Two weeks ago, scientists released a new study about TV viewing. The researchers found that kids who watched more than one hour of TV a day were more likely to show aggressive behavior as they grew older.

TV-Turnoff Network's goal is to encourage life outside the box. "We're not anti-TV," says Frank Vespe, director of the Network. The turnoff, says Vespe, will help kids tune into real life so that "they won't have time for TV."

Is it really possible to live without *SpongeBob SquarePants* and *The Powerpuff Girls*? Nathaniel Foote, 8, took part in TV-Turnoff last year. He says that "there are about 8,000 other things" to do. Think of how busy you'd be if you tried just 80 of those things!
—*By Kathryn R. Hoffman*

Hours in a year that the average American child watches television: **1,023**
Hours spent in school: **900**

Can you think of 20 things to do after school besides watch TV? Pair up with a friend and make a list.

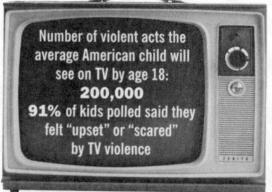

Number of violent acts the average American child will see on TV by age 18: **200,000**
91% of kids polled said they felt "upset" or "scared" by TV violence

Source: TV-Turnoff Network

go ▸ Join the TV turnoff! Print out a sign to cover your TV screen at *time forkids.com/turnoff*

TIME FOR KIDS

ONE BAD BUG!

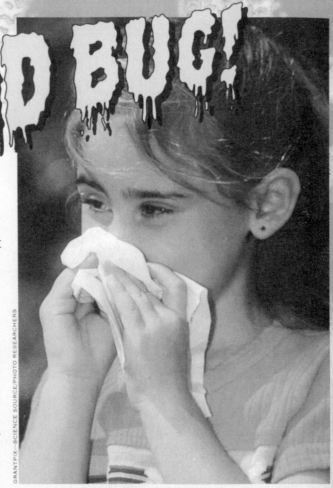

A runny nose and a cough are sometimes signs of the flu.

It's a sickness that slams you like a hammer. One minute you feel just fine. Next thing you know, you're shivering, then burning up. Your legs turn to jelly. Your body aches. No matter how much you hate bedtime, when you have the flu, you just want to go straight to bed.

Flu season lasts from November to April, and 31 states already have big outbreaks. Hospitals are packed. "I'm sending home twice as many kids as I usually do," says Jane Allen, a school nurse in Lubbock, Texas. Even in an ordinary flu season, 1 out of 10 Americans catches the bug.

"Children have the highest attack rate," says Dr. Carolyn Bridges of the Centers for Disease Control in Atlanta, Georgia.

Tiny Virus, Big Trouble

Like the common cold, influenza (flu, for short) is caused by a tiny virus. It spreads from person to person on the wet droplets of a cough or a sneeze. Once inside the body, the virus settles into the lining of the lungs, nose and throat. There the invaders make copies of themselves and spread farther.

A healthy person can usually fight off the flu in three to five days, but another sickness often follows. That's what happened to Phillip Winston, 10, of New City, New York. After a week, he finally beat the flu. "Then I got an ear infection," he says.

For elderly people and people who suffer from asthma and other illnesses, the flu can be dangerous. Doctors say these people should get a shot of flu vaccine every year.

Rest and drinking plenty of fluids are the keys to getting over the flu. And you should stay away from other people, warns Dr. Bridges. "It's not a nice thing to pass along to your friends." ■

The orange blobs on the page are pictures of flu viruses magnified many times.

FLU-FIGHTING TIPS

1. **Always cover your nose and mouth with a tissue when you cough or sneeze. Encourage everyone around you to do the same.**

2. **Wash your hands often, especially before eating.**

3. **Avoid rubbing your eyes or nose.**

4. **Don't share food or dishes with anyone. Even people who appear healthy can spread the flu virus.**

TIME FOR KIDS

hirsty and hot, 12 elephants plod across the fried African landscape. The water hole is less than a mile away now, and everyone in the **herd** is looking forward to a good, long drink. Tired **calves** want to stop, but mothers and aunts nudge them along. The older animals make soft, soothing noises. "We're almost there," they seem to say. "Just keep walking."

Suddenly everyone stops. Huge ears stretch out like satellite dishes. After a minute or two of what seems like silence, the animals turn and walk away from the water hole— fast. As they go, the adults huddle close to the calves.

So what happened? Why did the elephants change their course? They seemed to be listening to something. Whatever it was, they got the message to flee! Yet human ears heard nothing.

Elephants make plenty of sounds that humans can hear, such as barks, snorts, roars, and trumpet-like calls. Often a herd will use those sounds to talk with other elephants. But they weren't in the air this time.

SECOND LANGUAGE

For years, elephants puzzled observers with this type of behavior. But now scientists have solved the mystery. They discovered that elephants have a "secret" language for communicating over long distances. This special talk is based on **infrasound**, sounds so low in **pitch** that humans can't hear them. The sounds can travel several miles, allowing the six-ton animals to keep in touch across grasslands and forests in Africa or Asia.

To study elephant infrasound, researchers use special equipment that can record low-pitch sound waves. Another machine, called a **spectrograph**, translates the recorded sound waves into images, or markings, that we can see. The images stand for various messages.

▶ **Family Gathering.**
When danger lurks, adults huddle close to protect their calves.

▲ **Real Nose-y.**
With 50,000 muscles, an elephant's trunk works like a combination of arm, hand, and fingers.

CATHERINE PAYNE INSET:MICHAEL NICHOLS/NGS IMAGE COLLECTION

4

BIG TALKERS

Earth's largest land animals have a lot to say—even when they don't seem to be making a sound.

TEXT BY PETER WINKLER

5

Translating infrasound helps scientists begin to understand elephant behavior. For example, it turns out that the elephants heading to the water hole may have heard warning calls from another herd. Perhaps a lion was slurping water and looking hungry. The cat would be no match for an adult elephant, but it might kill a calf. No drink would be worth that risk, so the herd turned away.

▲ Trouble Ahead?
Lions sometimes attack elephant calves, so this elephant might warn herds to stay away.

Big Eater.
An adult can scarf down 300 pounds of leaves and grass in just one day.

LONG-DISTANCE CALLS

Elephants use infrasound to communicate many types of messages over long distances. Some of their talk helps hold families together. To understand how this works, you need to know a little about elephant families.

Females spend their lives with mothers, sisters, and children. They form tight-knit herds of 10 to 20 members. The oldest female elephant—the **matriarch**—takes charge. Males live with a herd until they are teenagers. Then they depart, living alone or joining with other males in a "bachelor herd."

The members of a herd often scatter over large areas to seek food for their mighty appetites. (An adult elephant can eat 300 pounds of grass and plants in a single day!) Long-distance calls let elephants know where their relatives are. And when the matriarch says, "Come here!" the herd gathers within minutes.

Like curious kittens, elephant calves sometimes wander off and get into trouble. When that happens, they cry for help. Adults respond with infrasound calls and other noises: "It's okay. We're coming to help you."

Adult males and females often live far apart, so they use infrasound to find each other at mating time. Females mate only once every four years or so. When a female is ready, she makes a special series of calls. Males who hear the calls storm toward her. Sometimes two or more males battle fiercely for a chance to court the female.

HEARING AIDS

Elephants tune in to all this talk with their large, powerful ears. An African elephant's ear can grow to be six feet long and four feet wide (Asian elephants have much smaller ears.) When straining to hear something, the animal turns toward the sound and opens its ears wide.

At the same time, the elephant may raise its trunk to sniff at the wind. Elephants have a

6

N.J. DENNIS/PHOTO RESEARCHERS

WWF—Elephant Style.
Playful and social, young elephants make a pair of Wild Wrestling Friends. Their muddy coats block heat and flies.

keen sense of smell. Odors may help them figure out what they're hearing.

Elephants may have yet another way of learning what's going on around them. Although scientists haven't proved it, some scientists think elephants can feel infrasound as the sound waves travel through the ground.

DISTRESS CALL

Communication skills help Earth's largest land animals survive in the wild. But even these skills can't save elephants from **extinction**.

In 1997 Africa's elephant population was about 500,000. That may seem like a lot, but there were 1.3 million African elephants in 1979. More than half of the elephant population vanished in only 18 years.

How did this happen? **Poachers** killed many elephants for their ivory tusks, because ivory can be sold for a lot of money.

And a growing human population wiped out vast amounts of elephant **habitat** to build farms and towns. Elephants from these areas wandered into human settlements. Some

elephants ate valuable crops and made some farmers angry enough to kill them.

HOW WILL WE ANSWER?

Conservationists are working hard to save elephants. Wildlife groups are trying to persuade people around the world to stop buying ivory.

Elephant supporters are also working with African communities to maintain parks where elephants can be safe and will not harm crops. Some conservationists hope that tourists will visit these beloved animals there. That would mean jobs for local people, who would then view elephants as a valuable resource to protect.

WORDWise ✕✕✕✕✕

calf: the young of some large animals, such as whales and elephants (plural: *calves*)

conservationist: a person who protects natural resources

extinction: the end of an entire species

habitat: the place where something lives

herd: a group of one type of animal that stays together

infrasound: sound so low that humans can't hear it

matriarch: a female who leads a herd

pitch: how high or low a sound is

poacher: one who kills or takes wild animals illegally

spectrograph: a machine that translates recorded sound waves into images

WebLink

More Elephant Talk

Reunite a young elephant with its mother by answering questions about Africa's biggest talkers. You'll find the "Lost Elephant" game on the NATIONAL GEOGRAPHIC FOR KIDS website at *www.nationalgeographic.com/ngforkids/links*.

7

ELEPHANTS IN AFRICA

NATIONAL GEOGRAPHIC

MAP OF THE MONTH

AFRICA

EUROPE

ASIA

Nile River

Nile River

Congo River

A

R

A

H

A

S

Niger River

ATLANTIC OCEAN

EQUATOR

ATLAS MOUNTAINS

8

Land Regions

Most of Africa is made up of high, flat land. There are few mountains. Deserts cover the northern and southern tips of the continent. Rain forests grow along the Equator. Grasslands called *savannas* fill most of the remaining land.

Elephant Population

We are not sure how many elephants live in Africa. It is very hard for humans to trudge through thick wilderness to find the animals. The counts we have are good guesses or estimates. These estimates include the number of elephants that people have spotted from the ground and the air. Some estimated numbers also come from elephant tracks and other clues.

Questions

1. Look at the map. In what land regions do most African elephants live?

____

2. Look at the population chart below. In which area of Africa are population counts the least definite? Why do you think that is?

____

Area	Definitely This Many	Probably This Many More	Possibly This Many More Still
Central Africa	7,320	81,657	128,648
Eastern Africa	90,292	16,707	20,190
Southern Africa	170,120	16,382	34,660
Western Africa	2,771	1,282	5,024

Source: International Union for Conservation of Nature and Natural Resources/African Elephant Specialist Group, 1997

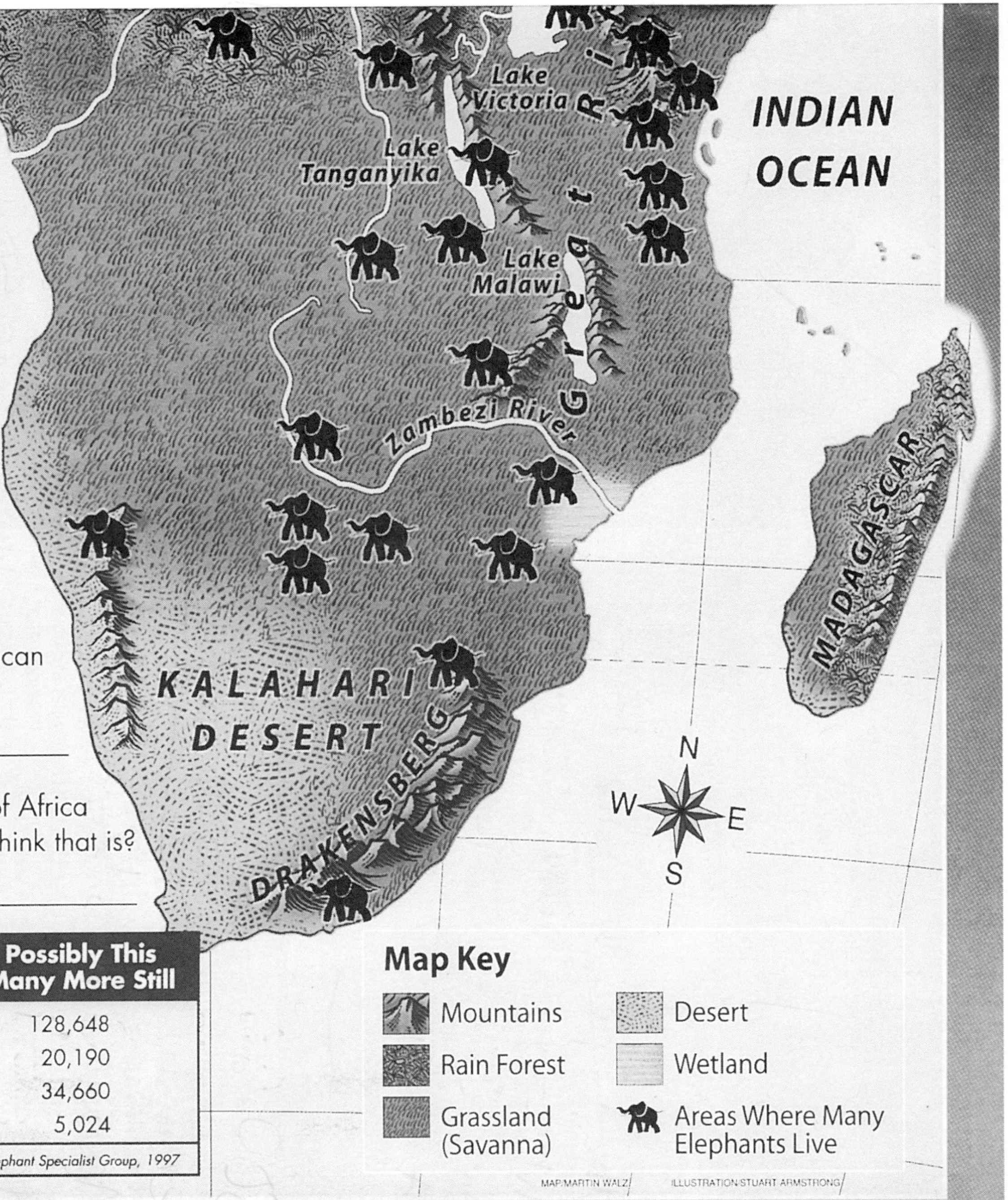
Lake Victoria
Lake Tanganyika
Lake Malawi
Great Rift
Zambezi River
INDIAN OCEAN
MADAGASCAR
KALAHARI DESERT
DRAKENSBERG
N
W
E
S
Map Key
Mountains
Rain Forest
Grassland (Savanna)
Desert
Wetland
Areas Where Many Elephants Live
MAP: MARTIN WALZ
ILLUSTRATION: STUART ARMSTRONG

9

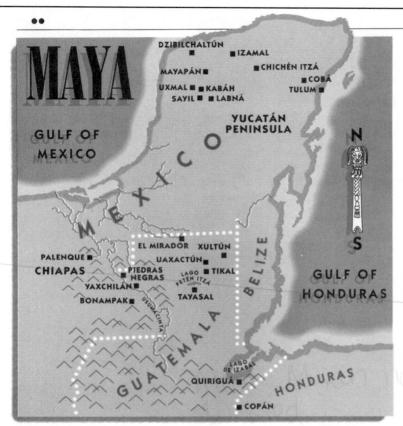

MAYA

DZIBILCHALTÚN ■ ■ IZAMAL
■ CHICHÉN ITZÁ
MAYAPÁN ■ ■ COBÁ
UXMAL ■ ■ KABÁH TULUM ■
SAYIL ■ ■ LABNÁ

GULF OF MEXICO

YUCATÁN PENINSULA

N / S

EL MIRADOR ■ ■ XULTÚN
PALENQUE ■ UAXACTÚN ■
CHIAPAS PIEDRAS ■ NEGRAS ■ TIKAL
LAGO PETÉN ITZÁ
YAXCHILÁN ■
BONAMPAK ■ TAYASAL

GULF OF HONDURAS

MEXICO · GUATEMALA · BELIZE · HONDURAS

LAGO DE IZABAL
QUIRIGUÁ ■
■ COPÁN

Thousands of years ago, not a single human being lived in all of North or South America. Then, around 23,000 B.C., the first people arrived from Asia. Slowly, they roamed south, and some settled in parts of Mexico, Central America, and South America. Later, they became known as the Maya.

From these humble beginnings, the Maya created one of the most splendid civilizations of all time. They erected magnificent palaces, developed an elaborate system of writing and an accurate calendar, and were able to predict eclipses.

Then, around A.D. 800, something terrible must have occurred. During the next century, many Maya cities became deserted. In time, the jungle once again claimed this Maya land.

Who were the Maya? What did they achieve? Journey back in time and witness one of the most fascinating—and puzzling—civilizations of all times.

▲ **THE MAYA LIVED** in an area of about 120,000 square miles. The heart of their civilization was the tropical rain forests in what are now the lowlands of northern Guatemala.

▲ **BLACK HOWLER** monkeys were considered sacred by the Maya. They served as gods of writing.

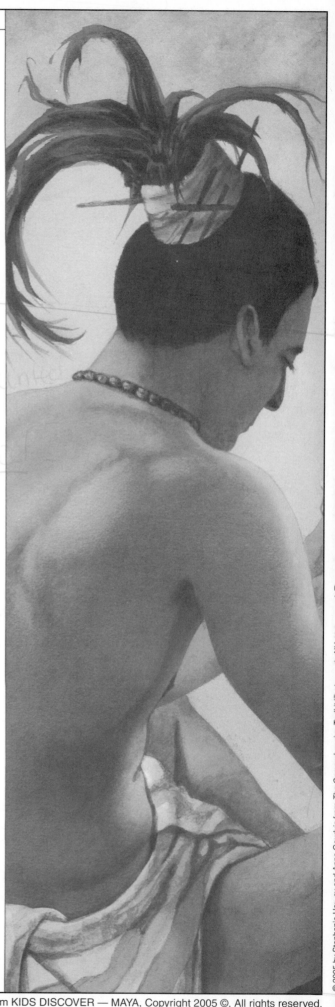

2

CHECK IT OUT!

The first Americans came from Asia to North America via a land bridge over the Bering Strait. That land bridge no longer exists. What do you think happened to it?

3

ARCHAEOLOGISTS (experts who study the remains of past cultures) often divide time into periods to make it easier to discuss history. Maya history is divided into three periods.

Archaic Period

7000 B.C. to 2000 B.C. Most Maya lived a hunting-and-gathering existence.

Preclassic Period

2000 B.C. to A.D. 250 Many Maya lived in settled communities.

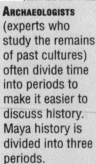

▲ **THE EARLIEST MAYA** lived in densely inhabited villages of high-pitched, thatched-roof houses.

WILD ANIMALS, ▲ such as deer, peccaries, tapirs, and monkeys, were hunted for food. Maize, beans, manioc, and squash, along with other crops, were cultivated outside the village. There were plenty of nuts, seeds, and wild fruits for the taking.

◄ **STATUES AND** carvings in many classic Maya cities show what the people looked like—or the looks they admired: straight black hair, high cheekbones, Oriental eyes, aquiline noses, and elongated skulls.

Early, Earlier, Earliest

There's a saying: "Rome was not built in one day." It means that it takes a long time to create something significant and lasting. This saying applies to the Maya.

The earliest Maya hunted animals, fished, and gathered wild berries, nuts, and seeds for food. By around 7000 B.C., these roving bands of Maya began making homes for themselves—in caves, rock shelters, and open camps. Slowly, over the next several thousand years, they began living a

Classic Period

A.D. 250 to 900 The Maya reached great heights in intellectual, artistic, and cultural areas. A class system existed, in which there were some rich and some poor people, some craftspeople and some farmers, and some religious leaders and some political leaders.

➤ **TWELVE-YEAR-OLD** Pacal came to the throne in the town of Palenque in A.D. 615. He reigned for 68 years. During his time the city became large and powerful. When Lord Pacal died, he had a royal burial in the Temple of the Inscriptions. The sarcophagus (coffin) lid shows Lord Pacal resting on a throne.

➤ **THE TALLEST STELA** (stone slab) in the Maya area—more than 30 feet high—is Stela F at Quiriguá, Guatamala. On it is a portrait of Cauac Sky, an important ruler in A.D. 724. Stelae were erected to honor the important events in leaders' lives.

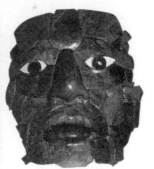

▲ **IMPORTANT PEOPLE** were buried in a seated position, along with pottery and other items. Platforms enclosed the tomb. Later burials and their platforms were placed over previous ones. This jade mask, found in a tomb, depicted a nobleman.

more settled village life. They wore animal-skin clothing and used flint-tipped spears.

As time went on, cities appeared, some containing as many as 75,000 people. The Maya reached great heights in the arts, scientific learning, architecture, and writing. Their economy flourished. Huge palaces, plazas, courtyards, and ball courts were erected. Towering temple-pyramids dotted the area.

5

THE INVENTIVE MAYA

MAY 9, 755

HE CAPTURED

JEWELED SKULL

2ND CAPTIVE

HIS CAPTIVE

BIRD JAGUAR

AT THE PLACE OF YAXCHILAN

2ND CAPTIVE   JEWELED SKULL

Ancient Astronomy

➤ THE MAYA'S knowledge of astronomy was very advanced. The Maya plotted the movements of the sun, moon, and Venus, and calculated the revolution of Venus around the sun as seen from the Earth to be 584 days. After many centuries of study, it has been determined that it is 583.92! This observatory is at Chichén Itzá.

▲ THE MAYA LEFT permanent records about their lives in hieroglyphs—pictures or symbols used to represent words, syllables, or sounds. Glyphs in books, on pots, carved in stone, and painted in murals show many aspects of Maya life, although most focus on important events in rulers' lives. Above is a record with the date of A.D. 755 on it, showing Bird Jaguar and a companion capturing Jeweled Skull and another enemy. Of all the people in the pre-Columbian Americas, only the Maya could write down anything they chose to in their own language.

▼ THE MAYA PAINTED and adorned their buildings with carved friezes, facades, and roof combs (extensions to make a building taller). Colorful murals adorned many interior walls. This structure is in Tikal, the largest of all classic sites.

▲ A FAVORITE ACTIVITY for kids was *pok-ol-pok*. This ball game was both a competitive sport and a sacred ceremony. The players tried to knock a solid rubber ball through a stone ring. The ball had to be bounced off the hips, shoulders, and forearms. The winners were entitled to the clothing and jewelry of the losing team!

▲ THE LONGEST single inscription in the Maya area is contained on the risers of these steps in the Hieroglyphic Stairway at Copán. More than 2,500 stones were used in constructing the risers, which tell the history of the ruling family.

▲ THE MOST REMARKABLE ASPECT OF the carvings is that they were done with stone tools—no metal was used in classic Maya times.

6

MAYA MATH MASTERY

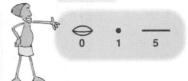

Dad, I'll *never* understand how to count!

It's not *that* tough, son. Just listen closely. We Maya were among the first to invent a way to count into really big numbers. We can count as high as we want because we know how important **nothing** is.

Nothing!?!

Zero, son. Only three peoples in all of history discovered it. Zero allows us to count until the iguana come home.

How, Dad?

The first thing you need to understand is that we use just three symbols for our numbers — a **shell** for zero, a **dot** for one, and a **bar** for five.

⌒	•	▬
0	1	5

We can count all the way to **nineteen** with those same symbols.

0	1	2	3	4
5	6	7	8	9
10	11	12	13	14
15	16	17	18	19

That makes sense.

Now, we Maya count in **steps**, as if walking down a stairway. On the lowest step are the numbers **1** through **19**. To show numbers from **20** to **399**, we go to the next step. A number on that step is 20 times what you think it is.

$$\text{•} = 120$$
$$\text{••••} = \underline{14}$$
$$134$$

We add the two steps to get the number and read the number from **top** to **bottom**, right?

You're a chip off the old block! Now, we stay on this step until we get as high as the number **399**. Then we have to step up again. The same process works for this step, except that you must figure 20 times 20 times the number, or 400 times the number you see.

$$\text{••} = 800$$
$$\text{•} = 120$$
$$\text{••••} = \underline{14}$$
$$934$$

I get it! Just keep stepping!

Step on! This step is good until you get to **7,999**.

So why is the zero so important, Dad?

Sometimes, son, it's important that there be nothing on a step. How could we write the number **403** without a zero?

$$\text{•} = 400$$
$$\text{⌒} = 0$$
$$\text{•••} = \underline{3}$$
$$403$$

▲ **MAYA BOOKS,** called codices, were long strips of paper made from the bark of the wild fig tree. The strips of bark were then folded back to back, forming pages, which may have been enclosed in covers of jaguar skin or wood.

▼ **THE LONG COUNT** is the Maya system of recording time. It is considered the most accurate calendar of the ancient world. Long Count calculations appear on most stelae from the classic period, helping archaeologists know when they were erected. One sign of Maya genius was their calculation of the true length of the year as 365.2420 days. The figure used today, after over 1,000 years of study, is 365.2422 days!

▲ **BONAMPAK IN** Chiapas, Mexico, was discovered in 1946. It contains many murals with scenes of 1,100 years ago. One room celebrates an heir to the throne. Glyphic captions explain the event and identify the people. Dancers in feather robes are moving to musicians' music. The second room shows war and a beheaded victim.

7

AFTER HERNANDO Cortés destroyed the Aztec realm in 1519, he and others went on to conquer the Maya. The Maya fought courageously but were finally subdued in the 1800s. The Spanish conquistadors, marching beneath the banner of "God, Glory, and Gold," accomplished their goal of subduing and wiping out the Maya and other cultures. Everyone was forced to take instruction in the Catholic faith. If anyone rebelled, the consequences were terrible.

THE SPANISH made slaves of many of the Indian peoples. They introduced such European diseases as smallpox, measles, and influenza to the Maya, who had no natural defenses against them. Entire towns were wiped out. Some estimate that up to ninety percent of the Maya died in the century immediately following the Spanish conquest.

LONG BEFORE THE Spanish arrived, Maya civilization was in decline. Civil unrest, social upheaval, and warfare were common. Few creative endeavors were pursued. In time, Mexican influence prevailed. Chichén Itzá is the place that best shows this. El Castillo, the Temple of the Jaguars and its Ball Court, and the Temple of the Warriors (right) incorporate elements that are totally different from Maya architecture: colonnades, rooms divided by columns, interior courts, and square platforms. It may be that the Toltec peoples of Mexico conquered the city.

The Spanish Conquest and the Decline of the Maya

Maya civilization flourished for many centuries. But then, from about A.D. 800 to 900, nearly all Maya cities in the southern lowlands were abandoned. Many theories have been proposed to explain this phenomenon: conquering armies of Mexicans, climatic changes, earthquakes, epidemics, economic failure, social disintegration, overpopulation and starvation, uprisings among the masses, or a combination of all these factors. A good guess is that a combination of outside pressures and internal tensions led to the collapse of the Maya.

Although the southern lowlands were nearly deserted, Maya splendor did continue in the Yucatán peninsula. When Spanish explor-

8

◀ **IN THE 16TH** century, Diego de Landa, a Franciscan friar from Spain, arrived in Yucatán, where Maya thrived after the lowland cities were abandoned. De Landa tried to change the ways of the Maya, but they refused to give up their beliefs. Angered, he had all their manuscripts burned, robbing future generations of valuable information about the Maya. In one terrible moment, de Landa wiped out the literature of an entire culture!

▼ **THE TOLTEC** Temple of the Warriors at Chichén Itzá, which is copied from a Mexican pyramid, clearly shows Toltec influence and ascendancy over the Yucatán.

Scribes Were Big Deals

SCRIBES RECORDED DETAILS ABOUT MAYA life on accordion-folded books. The pages of bark were strengthened by a natural gum substance and coated with white stucco. On these pages, scribes drew figures and made hieroglyphic symbols, coloring them with mineral and vegetable paints. Scribes, held in high esteem, also carved limestone, inscribed shells, and engraved jade.

▲ THE MONKEY-MAN SCRIBES

▲ RABBIT GOD WRITING A CODEX

ers set foot there in the early part of the 16th century, they found cities thronged with people, highly decorated palaces, temples raised on terraced pyramids, paved stone roads, and bustling marketplaces. They met leaders who wore jade and gold jewelry, intricate headdresses, jaguar-skin skirts, and brightly colored feathered capes. They also found warriors with bows, arrows, and clubs.

For years, the Spanish had been searching for the legendary El Dorado, where great riches were supposed to be found. The cities of the Maya could have been it. But the desire of the Spanish to convert others to their religion led ultimately to the destruction of the most brilliant civilization in pre-Columbian America.

9

Maya Today

Most of the more than six million modern Maya live in rural areas of Mexico, Guatemala, and Belize—areas where their ancestors lived. Their culture is a mixture of pre-Columbian Indian, European, and modern elements—not purely one or another.

The Maya today are not very well off economically. In the 1970s, the Guatemalan government began a systematic campaign to destroy Maya culture, killing thousands of highland Indians and forcing tens of thousands of others to flee across the border into Mexico. Entire villages have been razed to the ground and new ones built where the natives are forced to abandon their language, native dress, and local village organizations.

Will the Maya survive this latest onslaught or not? This remains to be seen.

➤ **IN REMOTE AND** isolated villages, houses are the same thatched-roof dwellings with lime-plas- tered stone or earthen walls that were used in classic times.

➤ **IN MANY PLACES,** traditional dress is common, but Maya also enjoy wearing colorful clothing from other cultures.

➤ **MAYA AUTHORITY** Linda Schele teaches modern Maya the writing of their ancestors.

➤ **MAYA LIFE TODAY** reflects the long history of outside influences. Nearly every town has a Catholic church, a public school, and municipal buildings. Some towns even have a movie theater, a tavern, and a gas station. Many Maya houses have radios and electric lights. On roads there are trucks, cars, and buses. Yet in spite of the inroads of other cultures, the Maya have clung to some original traditions.

10

MANY MAYA today resist attempts to make them part of the mainstream of Mexican and Guatemalan life. They don't want to be an oppressed minority. They cherish their own culture and values.

POTTERY IS STILL made by ancient methods. Traditional backstrap looms are used to make splendid fabrics.

AS IN PRE-Columbian times, adjacent structures serve as cooking or storage units, and the houses are grouped in compounds.

COLORFUL TEXTILES and ancient techniques of textile making survive in Guatemala and Chiapas. In Guatemala, the ancient calendar is still used to mark the annual ceremonial cycle.

MANY FESTIVALS and religious celebrations include such pre-Columbian activities as the burning of copal incense, fasting, and offerings.

RIGOBERTA MENCHÚ, a spokesperson for native peoples, won the Nobel Peace Prize in 1992.

11

The sun has not yet risen over the rocky hills outside the city of Peshawar, in Pakistan. Loudspeakers from the top of a **mosque** (mahsk), or **Muslim** house of worship, call out to the people, "God is great! It is better to pray than sleep! Come to prayers!"

Ten-year-old Garana rises from a mat on the dirt floor of her family's house. She puts on her black robe and covers her head with an old shawl. Then she walks to the mosque to pray.

Garana and her family have lived in their one-room house for two years. It's one of thousands of mud-brick homes in the Shamshatoo **Afghan** Refugee Camp. The camp holds about 50,000 Afghan **refugees**. They are people who have fled from war or **drought** in Afghanistan.

Garana works hard. Her father left the family several years ago. Her mother can't see very well and can do little to help. Her older brother works all day weaving carpets. And her younger brother is too small to do many chores. So Garana does most of the household tasks. But her day is not all work. She has time for school, friends, and even a little mischief.

Home Away From Home. *Garana (top left) lives in this refugee camp in Pakistan. Her family fled from war-torn Afghanistan two years ago.*

18

A day in the life of a
young Afghan refugee

Garana's Story

BY KENT PAGE

19

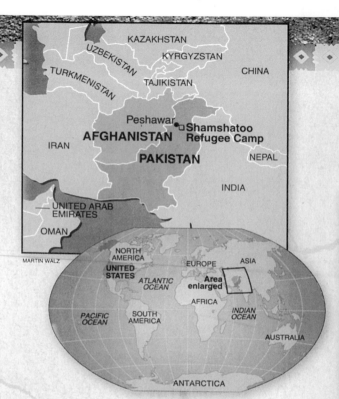

Weighty Experience. *Garana fetches water five or six times a day. She uses the full weight of her body to move the pump handle up and down.*

Early Morning

After prayers, Garana begins her morning chores. She walks to the camp's water pump to fill two bottles. After bringing them home, she eats breakfast, which is usually hot tea and bread. Then she washes the dishes in the backyard, using cold pump water. Next she sweeps the floor of the one-room house.

Then it's time to walk to the bakery. There she leaves a small amount of flour. The bakers will use it to make a loaf of bread. Garana's family will eat that loaf for their next three meals.

Now it's time to walk to school.

Class Time

Children in the refugee camp go to school six days a week. Boys and girls attend separate classes. Garana is in first grade, although she is ten years old. That's because when she lived in Afghanistan, Garana and other girls were not allowed to go to school. She has a lot of catching up to do. Classes in Garana's school go only through the second grade for girls

Follow the Letters. *Garana and her teacher guide the class through the English alphabet.*

and the third grade for boys. Still, it's an important start.

Garana gets to school just before classes begin at 8:30. The concrete building has six classrooms. These rooms have no windows, but there is paint on the walls.

20

Daily Bread. *Every day Garana gives local bakers some flour. They use it to make bread for her family.*

Thirty-five girls are in Garana's class. The students sit on mats on the floor. They study mathematics, the Afghan languages of Pashto and Dari, and the English alphabet. There is also class time for singing and drawing. Garana enjoys school.

"My favorite subject is English," she says. "If you can speak languages, then you can understand what people are saying. It's easier to get things done."

Today Garana stands at the chalkboard with a ruler and leads the class through the English alphabet. She mixes up *b* and *d*. Otherwise, she recites the alphabet perfectly.

Lunch Break

Classes end before lunch. The students race out to the small dirt playground to play on the swings, the slide, and the merry-go-round. Garana usually visits with her friends. But soon it's time for more chores.

She heads to the bakery to pick up the bread. Then she walks along the mud streets to her house. After a quick hello to her mother, Garana goes to the pump to collect water. When she returns, she fills the teapot and puts it on the small fire. Garana sits on her mat on the floor and eats her lunch with her hands. Today her mother has prepared potatoes along with the bread and tea.

"Some days we have potatoes. Some days we have rice. And some days we have beans," Garana says. "Whatever we eat for lunch, we have again for dinner. Rice is my favorite food."

Afternoon and Evening

After lunch, Garana trudges back to the pump for water to wash the plates and cups. Then she sweeps the house, cleans the yard, and feeds her family's four chickens. Once in a while, when there is money, she goes to the local shop to buy food. After she finishes her chores, she does her homework.

Soon it's time for dinner. Because the houses in the refugee camp have no electricity, the family eats the evening meal before it gets dark. Then, if there is any daylight left, Garana plays with her best friend, Assia. Sometimes they get into a little trouble.

"Garana saw some of the older girls with jewelry in their noses," Assia explains. "She said that looked beautiful. She asked me to pierce her nose. So I took a long sewing needle, and I did it."

Garana's mother was not pleased. But she helped Garana put a string through the hole to keep it open. Garana hopes that someday she can replace the string with jewelry.

21

A Wish for Peace

Garana has a hard life in the refugee camp. But at least there is no fighting. "I would like to go back to Afghanistan," she says. "but not until there is peace everywhere. We are told at school that some parts of Afghanistan are safe. But there is still fighting in other parts."

Many others share Garana's wish. For more than 20 years, the nation has suffered from war and unrest. Now the Afghan people, with the help of countries around the world, are trying to make changes. They hope to bring peace to Afghanistan.

Wordwise

Afghan: person from Afghanistan

drought: long period of time without rain or snow

mosque: Muslim place of worship

Muslim: one who practices the religion of Islam

refugees: people forced to flee their homes, usually to another country

High Hopes. *Garana and friend Assia (pink shirt) dream of returning to the mountains of Afghanistan (below).*

22

Back to School
Education = Hope for Afghan Children

It was March 25, 2002. Crowds of boys and girls gathered throughout Afghanistan. Excited whispers filled the air. Many children had waited and waited for this moment. The first day of school was about to begin!

Were these children really that happy to start school? The answer is yes. Many Afghan children hadn't attended school in years. Girls weren't allowed to go. And staying home seemed safer for some boys.

Many Afghan children were growing up without the skills they needed to earn a living. They faced lives of poverty. For them, school equals hope.

AMERICAN RED CROSS/DANIEL CIMA

Ready to Learn. *Afghan students hold new school supplies donated by kids in the United States.*

Class Acts

Unfortunately, years of fighting had destroyed or damaged 2,000 Afghan schools. The rest were in poor shape. And no one had money or materials to fix them.

So the United Nations Children's Fund (UNICEF) and American Red Cross pitched in. Working with Afghan leaders, they repaired broken windows and doors. They also bought new desks, chairs, chalkboards, and textbooks.

U.S. students helped too. They donated money that paid for chests full of school supplies. Afghan students got pencils, chalk, crayons, notebooks, rulers, jump ropes, and soccer balls.

No Complaints From This Crowd

All this help was just a start. Afghan schools still don't have space for every student. Classrooms are cramped, and tents hold extra classes.

To ease crowding, most schools have two shifts. Half the children attend morning classes. Others go in the afternoon. But Afghan students aren't complaining. They're just glad to be back.

"I never stopped thinking about the day when I might go back to school," says Safi, a nine-year-old girl. "And then one day I heard on the radio that school would start again. I was so happy."

— *Terrell Smith*

WebLink

Help Afghan Students

Find out what you can do at www.nationalgeographic.com/ngexplorer/articles.

23

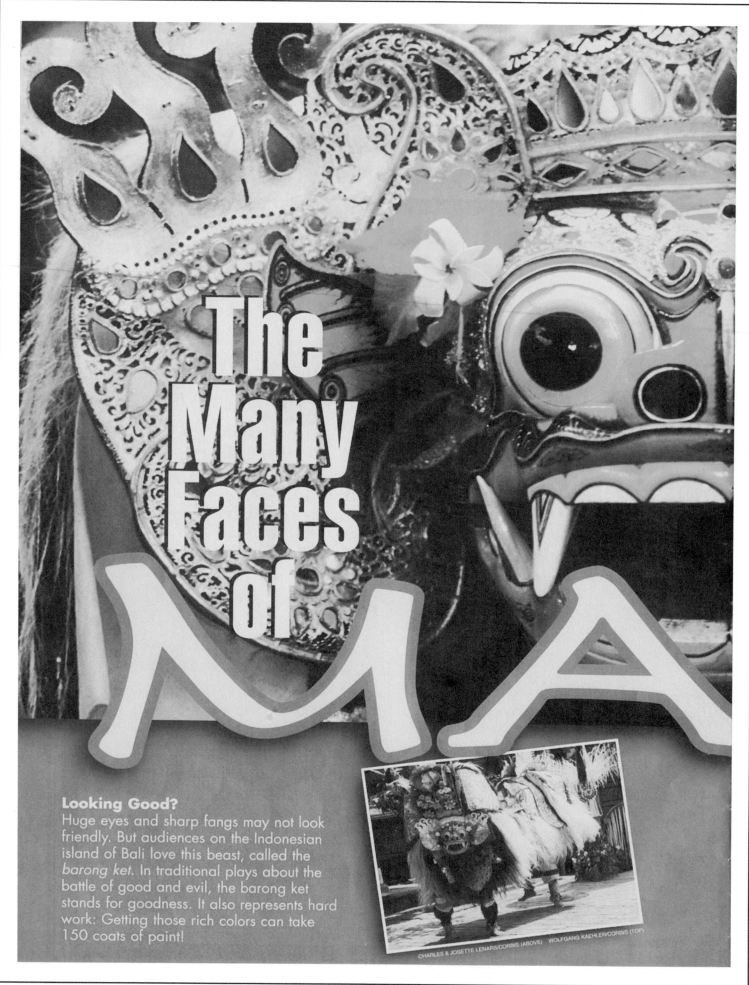

The Many Faces of MA

Looking Good?

Huge eyes and sharp fangs may not look friendly. But audiences on the Indonesian island of Bali love this beast, called the *barong ket*. In traditional plays about the battle of good and evil, the barong ket stands for goodness. It also represents hard work: Getting those rich colors can take 150 coats of paint!

CHARLES & JOSETTE LENARS/CORBIS (ABOVE)   WOLFGANG KAEHLER/CORBIS (TOP)

MASKS

BY JACKIE GLASTHAL

Put on a mask, and suddenly you're someone else. You become Harry Potter, Princess Fiona, a cat, a crook, or a clown. Masks change the way you look *and* feel. No wonder people sometimes think that masks have special powers!

For about 15,000 years, humans have created masks to use in storytelling, prayer services, death rituals, and more. This photo-essay brings you face-to-face with masks from around the globe. And it tells some of the stories behind the masks.

   81

Eyes on the AFTERLIFE

Ancient Egyptians designed this mask to look like their young pharaoh, or ruler—Tutankhamun (TOOT on kah mun). You may know him as King Tut. When Tut died in 1323 B.C., priests carefully **mummified** his body. Then they placed this golden mask over his face.

Why bury such a beautiful object? The answer lies in religion. Ancient Egyptians believed that when Tut died, his soul left his body and split into pieces. Some of those pieces returned to the body. The mask might help them find Tut.

The Inca people of South America also made burial masks from gold, wood, or clay.

Ancient Romans sometimes created a wax mask when someone died. They hired an actor to wear it during the funeral march.

CHARLES GRAHAM/STOCK PHOTOGRAPHY/PICTUREQUEST

PLAYING Around

When the ancient Greeks went to the theater 2,500 or so years ago, they never saw the actors' faces. Performers wore masks made of linen. Later they used leather too. The masks helped actors look like Zeus, Athena, and the other gods and goddesses who appeared in Greek plays. This was helpful because men played all the parts—even those of women.

We're not sure exactly what those masks looked like, but this sculpture of the river god Achelous (ak uh LOW us) gives you a rough idea. Some Greek masks had built-in **megaphones** to make the actor's voice louder.

RUGERRO VANNI/CORBIS

Let It RAIN!

The Nahua people living along the coast of Mexico crafted this mask of a rain god. The god's eyes are blue, like water in a lake. His hair and beard ripple like a stream.

The Nahua's rain gods seemed to sleep through long, dry winters. To wake them up in the spring, Nahua boys put on masks like this and danced on a mountainside. They performed this ritual into the 1800s.

Native peoples use masks in similar **ceremonies** today. The Hopi and Zuni tribes in the Southwest create fancy leather masks that stand for rain, stars, sky, and more.

In the Northeast, Iroquois healers wear wooden "false faces" with bulging eyes and broken noses. They believe the masks scare away illness and evil spirits.

CATALOGUE NO. 419925, DEPARTMENT OF ANTHROPOLOGY, SMITHSONIAN INSTITUTION

FAMILY Reunion

Family gatherings aren't just for the living. That's the view of the Yoruba people in western Africa. Villages hold special ceremonies to honor their ancestors. In exchange, the dead relatives are supposed to protect the living from harm.

For these ceremonies, the Yoruba create elaborate costumes and masks. Dancers wear these outfits to represent the ancestors' spirits. (But the masks are not portraits.) Relatives greet the spirits respectfully, hoping to make them feel like happy members of the family.

BOWERS MUSEUM OF CULTURAL ART/CORBIS

HARD AT

Many kids in Ecuador go to work instead of school

TEN-YEAR-OLD WILBUR CARreño is less than four feet tall and weighs only 50 pounds. He is small for his age. That's exactly what makes him good at his job.

Wilbur spends his afternoons climbing banana trees four times his height. He expertly ties the heavy stalks of bananas so the trees won't droop from the weight of the fruit. "I've been working since I was 8," he told TFK. "I finish school at noon and then go to the field."

In Wilbur's poor country of Ecuador, one in every four children is working. An estimated 69,000 kids toil away on the vast banana plantations along the country's coast. Ecuador is the word's largest banana exporter. Kids working in the industry are exposed to harmful chemicals, pull loads twice their weight and use sharp, heavy knives.

DO KIDS BELONG ON THE JOB?

Child labor is certainly not limited to Ecuador. The United Nations estimates that 250 million kids around the world are forced to work. Many countries don't have laws limiting kids' work.

A concerned group called Human Rights Watch conducted a study of Ecuador's banana plantations last April. They found that most children begin working on plantations around age 10. Their average workday lasts 12 hours! By age 14, 6 out of 10 no longer attend school. Many families face the difficult choice of either putting food on their tables or sending their kids to school.

The family of Alejandro, 12, struggles with that choice. Alejandro has had to work beside his father, Eduardo Sinchi, on a plantation. "I don't want my kids to work," says Sinchi. "I want them in school, but we have few options." Sinchi has nine children and earns as little as $27 a week. "It isn't even enough for food, let alone school, clothes, transportation."

HARD WORK FOR LITTLE PAY

Sinchi's pay is typical in Ecuador. The average banana worker earns just $6 a day. One reason pay is so low is that Ecuadorians are not allowed to form work groups called unions. In countries like Costa Rica, where laws allow unions, some banana workers earn $11 a day. Such countries have fewer child workers because better pay means parents can afford to keep their kids in school.

A 12-year-old boy pulls banana stalks on a metal runner after the fruit has been picked. He works up to 12 hours a day.

This boy makes up to 1,200 boxes a day. They are used to ship bananas to the U.S.

ZOE SELSKY (2)

WORK

Ecuador's big banana companies have begun to do something about child labor. Last year, they signed an agreement not to hire kids younger than 15 and to protect young workers from chemicals. "We need to eliminate child labor," says Jorge Illingworth, of Ecuador's Banana Exporters Association. But small plantations did not sign the agreement, and, he says, they employ 70% of the kids.

Banning child labor is a start, but it doesn't really help families like the Sinchis. Now that Alejandro can't work, his family suffers more. The answer, most believe, is better pay for Ecuador's adult workers. For that to happen, U.S. shoppers would have to put up with higher banana prices or stop buying Ecuador's bananas to make their point. Guillermo Touma fights to help Ecuador's workers. "If we could raise awareness," he says, "we could raise wages and invest in education for our children." —*By Ritu Upadhyay. Reported by Lucien Chauvin/Ecuador*

go For more information on how to get involved in campaigns against child-labor abuses, go to *timeforkids.com/labor*

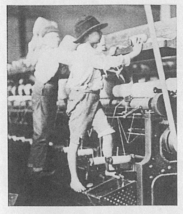

Child Labor in the U.S.A.

The mistreatment of child workers is not just a foreign problem. Throughout its history, the United States has counted on kids to lend a hand in fields and factories. In the 1800s, children as young as 7 worked in textile mills for 12 hours a day. By the end of the 19th century, almost 2 million kids performed hazardous jobs in mills, mines and factories.

Many concerned citizens worked to change this. Photographer Lewis Hine, who took this photo of young cotton mill workers, was one of them. In 1938, a U.S. law was passed that limits work hours for kids and requires safe conditions. The law still exists, but it is not always enforced. An estimated 800,000 children work illegally in the U.S. today, mostly in farming and related industries. Some work with heavy machinery, poisonous chemicals or under other conditions that could harm them.

Slim Pickings

Ecuador supplies a quarter of the bananas sold in the U.S. Most of the money from sales goes to U.S. grocery stores. Workers in Ecuador get little money. Here's about how much a 43-pound crate costs as it goes from the plantation to you.

■ **$2.40** Amount per crate a U.S. distributor pays banana exporters in Ecuador. Of this, about **$1.54** goes to plantation workers.

■ **$7.50** What supermarkets pay a distributor for a crate

■ **$22** What you would pay for 43 pounds of bananas at the grocery store

They're back!

Today, about 30,000 humpback whales roam our oceans. That's 30 times more than in 1965.

The Comeback H

COVER PHOTO/FLIP NICKLIN

Humpback whales are great acrobats. Using their powerful black-and-white speckled tails, they leap out of the water and flop on their backs. This is called **breaching**. Sometimes they even do somersaults. Spotting one of these giant gymnasts was harder 30 years ago. Humans had been hunting them for hundreds of years, and they were becoming **extinct**. Now, thanks to recent laws that protect humpbacks from hunters, these whales are making a long awaited comeback. That means that scientists are getting a better chance to study the humpback's amazing feats.

And amazing they are. A humpback's tail has to be very strong to launch it out of the water because a humpback weighs about 40 tons. That's the same weight as about eight male African elephants. When a humpback breaches, it flings out its front **flippers** almost as if it were going to fly. Its flippers measure up to 17 feet, which is as long as a canoe.

Humpbacks aren't the largest of all whales, but they are really big. From head to tail, they measure more than 40 feet. Humpbacks got their name from a hump that appears on a back **fin**. They also flex their backs up in a hump before they dive.

Water Wings.
When a humpback breaches, it flings out its front flippers as if it were going to fly.

Humpbacks

PHOTO/FRANÇOIS GOHER / PHOTO RESEARCHERS

Flying Leaps

Why do humpbacks breach? No one is quite sure. Some scientists say humpbacks breach because it helps them get rid of whale lice and **barnacles**. Barnacles are tiny shellfish that bore headfirst into their skin. When humpbacks slap their big bodies down on the water after breaching—whack—goodbye, pests! (They hope.)

Some scientists think humpbacks breach to threaten smaller whales with their big size. Still other scientists believe they do it to communicate with each other. Maybe there isn't just one answer.

Deep-Sea Singing

Humpbacks seem to communicate in another way—by "singing." Other types of whales also sing. The blue whale, which is the world's largest type of whale, has the loudest song. It belts out a tune that is thousands of times louder than a jumbo jet taking off.

But a loud song isn't everything. Scientists think the humpbacks sing very complex songs. The songs can go on for 30 minutes or so and sound to us like moans, groans, roars, squeaks, chirps, yups, and oohs. Just as people from various areas speak with distinct accents, humpbacks from different places have their

SEPTEMBER 2000

5

own special accents.

Only male humpbacks sing, and we're not sure why. The songs may have something to do with courting females because when a male attracts a female, he pipes down.

Coming Up for Air

You may be surprised to learn that whales are not fish. They are mammals. Instead of breathing through gills, they breathe through lungs like other mammals. A humpback can stay underwater for hours. Eventually it comes to the surface where it blows old air out of two **blowholes** on top of its head. It breathes in fresh air and dives back under.

Going the Distance

Humpbacks are great travelers. Every year they swim between their summer grounds where they feed and their winter grounds where they breed and raise their young. (See map on page 8.) Some travel as far as 5,000 miles one way. This movement is called **migration**.

Humpbacks live in both hemispheres of the world. In the Southern Hemisphere, they feed in waters around Antarctica. There the whales stock up on small fish and their great favorite—**krill**. Krill are shrimplike creatures that aren't much bigger than pieces of pop-corn. How does an animal as huge as a whale live on something so small? The answer is it eats a LOT of krill—maybe up to 4,400 pounds

Underarm Protection.
Mother humpbacks often tuck their babies under their big flippers to protect them. Babies weigh more than two tons when they're born.

◁ **Munch a Bunch of Krill.**
Popcorn-size krill are favorite whale food. Humpbacks can eat up to 4,400 pounds of them per meal.

during one meal. To reproduce, Southern Hemisphere humpbacks migrate north toward the Equator.

In the Northern Hemisphere, there are several groups of humpbacks. One favorite feeding ground is Glacier Bay near the Arctic Ocean. A group of humpbacks migrates from there to the warm Pacific waters of Hawaii. Many others feed in the North Atlantic Ocean and swim to the West Indies to mate and give birth.

6

Hunting for Humpbacks

Humpbacks are very curious. They often swim up to boats to check things out. This makes them easy to hunt. Fishermen began hunting humpbacks in Japan in the early 1600s and in eastern North America in the 1700s. They hunted them for their **blubber**, a thick layer of fat under their skin. Fishermen could eat the blubber as well as turn it into oil.

Fishermen also wanted the humpbacks' **baleen**. These are stiff strips that hang like a big comb in its jaws and take the place of teeth. When a humpback takes a big gulp of ocean, the baleen strains out the water and traps masses of krill and little fish. Businesses wanted baleen to make ladies' corsets. In the 1800s and 1900s, fishermen built big whaling stations on islands in Antarctica. Soon the numbers of humpbacks in the Southern Hemisphere began to decline, too.

To the Rescue

Scientists think that before whaling became popular, there were about 100,000 humpbacks in the world. By 1965 only 1,000 humpback whales remained. In 1966, humans realized that humpbacks and other whales were going to become extinct unless they did something. By the 1970s, humpbacks were put on the endangered species list as well as on other lists that protected them from hunters. Now scientists estimate that 30,000 humpbacks roam the seas. That is not close to what their worldwide population once was, but it is much larger than in 1965. It is probably enough to call the humpback "The Comeback Kid."

WebLink

Hear for Yourself!
Listen to a humpback sing at http://metalab.unc.edu/pub/multimedia/sun%2Dsounds/whales.

Unsolved MYSTERIES

1 Why do you think whales breach?

2 Why do you think they sing in different accents?

3 Do you think whales and birds sing for the same reasons?

Swim Up to the Mike. This humpback sings a moanful song into a recorder called a hydrophone. The white bumps on its flipper are barnacles.

PHOTO:FLIP NICKLIN

Whale Words

baleen: Stiff strips that hang like a big comb in the jaws of some whales. These strips take the place of teeth.

barnacle: A tiny hard-shelled animal that attaches itself to whales, rocks, and other sea surfaces.

blowhole: A nostril at the top of a whale's head. Humpbacks have two. Some whales have only one.

blubber: A thick layer of fat under a whale's skin.

breaching: Leaping out of the water.

extinct: No longer alive on Earth.

fin: A fan-shaped body part used to steer in water.

flipper: A broad, flat limb used for swimming.

krill: Small shrimplike creatures that whales eat.

migration: When animals move to a different area to avoid cold weather, find food, or find a safe place to breed and raise their young.

7

Answers to **CHECK IT OUT!** questions from Kids Discover – *Titanic* (pages 20–31)

Q: Where does the name RMS Titanic come from?
A: Titanic was a British ship, and the initials RMS stand for Royal Mail Steamship. Titanic means "big," after the Titans, a group of Greek gods famous for their size and strength. Titanic was also called SS (Steam Ship) Titanic.

Q: Did anyone predict the Titanic's sinking?
A: After the Titanic sank, many people said they had predicted the event. There is no hard evidence for these claims, but in 1898, Morgan Robertson published a novel called Futility, about an ocean liner called the Titan. In his story, the Titan is the biggest ship afloat when it strikes an iceberg and sinks in the North Atlantic. Most of the Titan's three thousand passengers die because there aren't enough lifeboats.

Q: Can hypothermia ever save lives?
A: Yes. Doctors often bring on hypothermia deliberately when performing brain or open-heart surgery. Their goal is to stop the circulation of blood. Without oxygen from blood, the brain would be permanently damaged within three to five minutes at normal temperatures. But during deep hypothermia, blood flow can be stopped naturally for an hour or longer and the patient can be safely revived.

Q: What happened to Titanic's sister ships?
A: Olympic had a distinguished career that ended in 1935, when it was sold and scrapped. Because Gigantic sounded too much like Titanic, the ship's name was changed to Britannic. It became a hospital ship at the outbreak of World War I. In 1916, it sank near Greece, apparently after hitting a mine. Twenty-one people died.

Answer to **CHECK IT OUT!** question from Kids Discover – *Maya* (pages 64–73)

Q: The first Americans came from Asia to North America via a land bridge over the Bering Strait. That land bridge no longer exists. What do you think happened to it?
A: Because it was the Ice Age and much of the land was frozen, the water level of the oceans was low. Land that is now covered with water was then exposed.

The Source Book
OF SHORT TEXT

Short Text Titles
and Reading Level Designations

KEY:
* Most Accessible text
** More Challenging Text
*** Most Challenging Text—Good selections for
teachers to model their own reading process and
for readers who want and need more of a challenge.

The First Olympics

The Olympics we know include many athletic events—basketball, swimming, sprinting, skating, and javelin throwing to name just a few. Athletes compete from all over the world.

But what if the Olympics had just one event and all of the athletes were from one country? That's exactly what is was like at the first ever Olympics, held in Olympia, Greece, in 776 B.C., more than 2,700 years ago.

The only event was a foot race, called a *stade,* and all of the athletes were from Greece. At the completion of the race cheering spectators threw flowers, and the judge placed an olive-branch wreath on the head of the proud winner.

For nearly 1,200 years after these first Olympics, the games took place every four years. The period between games was called an *Olympiad.* But in 393 A.D., Byzantine Emperor Theodosius I abolished them, along with all festivals.

Fifteen hundred years passed before the Olympic games returned, in 1896. They were still held in Greece and featured competitors from fourteen countries, including the United States. New events such as cycling, fencing,

The Olympic torch burns during each Olympics

swimming, and weightlifting were added. These were the first modern Olympics.

The Olympics continue today, summer and winter, every four years, in different countries around the world. They still combine the traditions of the ancient games, like the proud march into the stadium, but have incorporated traditions established during the modern games, like awarding medals to the winners. ■

Buried Alive!

It was August 26 and the people of Pompeii were going about their business, visiting local shops and doing their chores, when they suddenly heard loud rumblings. They looked up at the massive mountain that towered over their city and saw hot waves of volcanic ash pouring down the mountainside. They stopped what they were doing and fled.

Mount Vesuvius, as it overlooks Pompeii

The Great Cover-Up

The year was 79 A.D. and the eruption was coming from Mount Vesuvius, a 4,200-feet high volcano that today looks down upon the city of Naples, Italy. Over the past two thousand years, Vesuvius has erupted several times, most recently in 1944, but never was the damage as great as it was on that summer day in 79 A.D. The city of Pompeii and the nearby town of Herculaneum were buried under ten feet of the volcanic ash; only the rooftops of a few buildings remained visible.

It is believed that most of the twenty thousand people of Pompeii escaped the wrath of the mighty volcano. Days later, many of the citizens returned to where the city once stood. They started digging, trying to recover their valuables, but the task was too difficult, so they gave up.

An Amazing Discovery

For centuries Pompeii remained a lost and forgotten city. Then, in the year 1748, a peasant struck a buried wall while digging in his vineyard. Thus began the archeological excavations of the lost city that have continued ever since.

Viewing History

In the beginning of the excavation, valuable treasures were discovered and taken to a museum in Naples. But as the workers continued to dig, they discovered that most of the ancient city was still intact. The volcanic ash had preserved the city. Buildings still stood along streets, swords and armor worn by gladiators were found, kettles and jars stood in kitchens, bronze tools were found inside shops.

Today, you can tour the lost city of Pompeii, and much of Herculaneum has also been unearthed and can be viewed. The buildings, the streets, and even the graffiti on the walls illustrate what life was like at the moment Vesuvius erupted, nearly two thousand years ago. ■

The Great Depression: Mired in Poverty

Herbert Hoover was elected president of the United States in 1928. In his victory speech he said, "We in America today are nearer to the final triumph over poverty than ever before in the history of any land. The poorhouse is vanishing among us."

Less than a year later, in October of 1929, the stock market crashed. Many people lost their life savings. Businesses and banks closed, and people didn't have jobs. Suddenly there were more poor Americans than ever before.

The Great Depression lasted until the end of World War II, in 1945—almost seventeen years of national struggle. The United States' economic depression began to affect the entire world. Some feel it helped dictators like Adolf Hitler come to power. People were desperate to have their lives get better.

Day-to-day life was not good. Things were even worse for people in the middle part of the United States. In 1931 and 1932 there was a long drought; the Midwest and the South became known

The Great Depression lasted from 1929 – 1945

as the Dust Bowl. A lot of farmers had borrowed a lot of money to buy equipment. Now they couldn't sell their crops and couldn't pay back the money.

It was a hard time that people who lived through would remember all their lives. Members of the Great Depression generation often grew up to be frugal, hardworking people who saved their money and distrusted banks! They would never forget what it was like to be constantly hungry and to go without the things they needed and wanted. ■

Riding the Rails to Hope

Between 1854 and 1929 thousands of children were sent by train to parts of the United States far from where they lived. They rode what were called the *orphan trains.* Many of these children no longer had parents, or had parents who were too poor or otherwise unable to take care of them. Some were the children of immigrant parents who were unable to find work in a new land. As a result, many of these children were living on the streets.

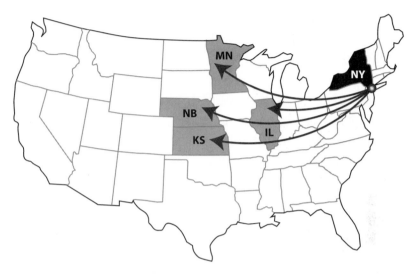

Orphan trains brought 200,000 children from New York City to the Midwest between 1854 and 1929.

Good Homes

The goal of the orphan trains was to save the growing number of these children from the streets of New York City and place them with loving, caring families in the Midwest who could take good care of them.

During the seventy-five years that the orphan trains ran, between 150,000 and 200,000 children were placed in homes in Kansas, Illinois, Nebraska, and many other states. Some were even placed in homes in Canada and Mexico.

The orphan trains brought many of these children to good, loving homes where they were legally adopted and treated very well. Two governors, a United States congressman, and many lawyers and bankers were once riders of the orphan trains.

Bad Homes

Unfortunately, many other children found that their new life was not very good. Many farmers made them work long hours on their farms. There are stories of children who were treated badly and abused. Some even ran away from their new homes, never to be heard from again. Famous teenage outlaw Billy the Kid rode the orphan train as a child.

New Options

Public reaction to the orphan trains was mixed. Some people thought it was a wonderful way of helping poor children. Other people thought it was a terrible way of turning children into workers. The government responded by creating new child labor laws during the 1920s. Then, in the late 1920s, new government programs were created to help children who were orphaned or from poor homes. This put an end to the orphan trains.

Today, there are foster-care agencies in every state that help abandoned or abused children find foster homes and sometimes adoptive families. ■

Navajo Code Talkers

By the time The United States entered World War II in 1941, Native Americans had been forced onto tracts of land called *reservations*. Indian children who went to school had long ago been forbidden from speaking their native languages and forced to use English.

But one of those very same forbidden languages would become a key to the United States success in the Pacific theater of World War II. The Japanese were intercepting and translating English messages, making strategy difficult. The U.S. military needed a code that the Japanese did not know.

The language of the Navajo became that code. Navajo was perfect for several reasons: 1) at the time there were no Navajo living outside the United States who could become translators for the enemy; 2) the Navajo language had not yet been studied by linguists; 3) Navajo is a unique, complex language; 4) Navajo is difficult to pronounce; and 5) Navajo did not have a written dictionary.

Young Navajo men were recruited as Marine Corps Radio Operators. Their work was considered by many to have been the

World War II Navajo Code Talker

key to the U.S. success in many World War II battles. But since the Code Talkers were sworn to secrecy, when they came home at the end of the war no one knew what they had done and they could not talk about it.

Finally, in 2000, they were awarded the Congressional Gold Medals from the U.S. Congress. The Code Talkers were credited with saving countless lives and winning many battles. The Navajo code became one of the most important and most successful military codes ever used. ∎

The Japanese-American Internment

The Japanese Imperial Navy launched a surprise attack on the United States on December 7, 1941. In two air strikes, Japanese planes bombed the Pearl Harbor Naval Base, in Hawaii, killing more than two thousand people. World War II was already raging in other parts of the world, but the United States had not entered the war. Until then.

Mess line, noon, Manzanar Relocation Center, California

Forced Evacuation

The United States military declared the West Coast a military zone and forced Japanese and Japanese Americans living on California's coast to evacuate. They said they had to do this because some of these people might be spies for Japan. They said it would help them discover Japanese spies. They said it was for the Japanese Americans' personal safety. And they said it had nothing to do with racial discrimination. Not everyone agreed.

Most of the thousands of Japanese nationals cooperated, packing up a few of their belongings and reporting to places like the Santa Anita horseracing track, near Los Angeles, California. People slept in horse stalls while they waited to be transported by the military to "camps" away from the coast. Men went first in order to construct the camps, which were like small towns with barber shops, hospitals, schools, and a recreation center every forty-eight blocks.

Protecting Citizen's Rights

The people of the United States were so angry with Japan for its actions that many thought this evacuation, called *internment* because it was forced confinement during time of war, was necessary. But members of two groups—the Quakers and the American Civil Liberties Union—spoke out against the internment as a violation of U. S. citizens' constitutional right of personal freedom.

Freedom at Last

Interned Japanese Americans were allowed to return home in 1944, a few months after the end of World War II. In 1948, the government paid them ten cents for every dollar they had lost when they were forced to leave their homes, their belongings, and their jobs. The descendents of the Japanese Americans who were interned during World War II received $20,000 under the Civil Liberties Act of 1988. Some people wonder if these payments, called *restitution,* even begin to make up what was lost. ■

The Passion of Cesar Chavez

School was difficult for Cesar Chavez. Cesar spoke only Spanish at home, but no one was allowed to speak Spanish at the American schools he attended. After his family moved from Arizona to California, Cesar's father had an accident and could no longer work. Cesar decided he had had enough of school and became a migrant farm worker instead of going to high school.

Although he did not have a lot of formal schooling, Cesar educated himself in things he felt were important to his life. Chavez created the National Farm Workers Association, later called the United Farm Workers Association. The UFW exists today as an important union for all farm workers.

Chavez learned about nonviolent protest, and those were the methods he chose—picket lines, boycotts, and fasts—to gain recognition for the importance and dignity of farm workers.

His nonviolent protests included several long fasts, one for thirty-six days with just water. "Fasting for life" became a fast picked up for three days at a time by famous people such as Reverend Jesse

Jackson, actor Martin Sheen, and singer Carly Simon. Chavez wanted to protect farm workers from pesticides and the loss of their rights. And he wanted to prove that violence was not necessary to gain rights.

Cesar Chavez died peacefully in his sleep, at age sixty-six, after a long day in court testifying in defense of the UFW for a successful lettuce boycott. His name will always be associated with the rights of laborers. ■

Boycott for Change

In the 1880s a man named Charles Boycott was in charge of an estate in Ireland when a politician declared that all landlords must lower the rents they charged people living on their land. Boycott refused to do so. As a result, the politician saw to it that no one would have anything to do with Boycott. His servants would no longer work for him. Clerks in stores refused to wait on him. Even the mail carriers refused to deliver his mail.

As a result of what happened to Charles Boycott, the word boycott is used to describe the action of people joining together to send a message by not buying a certain product or refusing to deal with a business, group, or an entire nation.

How to Boycott

For example, if a store decided to expand by building in a park where many children like to play, you might ask all the families in the neighborhood to boycott that store by not shopping there. This would hurt the store's business and let the owners know that the people do not agree with their plan to take away the playground.

Famous Boycotts

There have been many famous boycotts in history. In 1955, when African Americans were only allowed to sit in the back seats on busses in Montgomery, Alabama, Dr. Martin Luther King organized a boycott of the Montgomery busses. African Americans did not ride the busses for nearly a year until the law was changed and people of all races could sit wherever they chose on the busses.

Boycotts have helped improve the conditions for migrant workers such as these.

In the 1960s and 1970s, when grape pickers and migrant farm workers were being underpaid, organizations urged the people of the United States to boycott grapes and lettuce. Many people did not buy either product until finally the grape pickers and migrant workers were given more money.

In 1980, many nations boycotted the Moscow Olympics (in the Soviet Union) by not sending their athletes as a protest against the Soviet Union's invasion of Afghanistan in 1979.

When a cause is supported by many people, a boycott can be a very successful means of sending a message. ■

The Case Against Soda

Soda. Pop. Soda pop. Whatever you call it, those sugary, fizzy drinks that the world has come to love are not very good for you. Why not?

First, they can cause you to put on the pounds. A typical can of soda (sixteen ounces) contains 207 calories. Drinks are often forgotten as a calorie source, and it's easy to get 500 calories a day from a couple of cans of soda. That's around one fourth of your daily caloric needs that you don't even notice! And that doesn't give you any nutrition.

Then, they're bad for your teeth. Sugar is known to cause tooth decay. So the more soda you drink, the more likely you'll be spending a lot of quality time with your dentist.

If that's not enough, there are hidden dangers. Soda contains something called phosphoric acid—that's what makes it fizzy. Too much phosphoric acid can cause an imbalance of the minerals calcium and phosphorus in your body. That imbalance is bad for the growth and strength of your bones.

How are kids to make good decisions about what to drink when the soda companies pay their schools to put soda machines right in the hall? That practice may be coming to an end! Several states have passed laws limiting or eliminating vending machines in schools.

Like everything related to food and drink, moderation is best. Having a soda now and then isn't going to hurt you! But several cans of soda every day is not good for your health. ■

Influential Advertising

Have you ever stopped to think how many places you see advertisements for products to buy, places to visit, or movies to see? Sure, there are plenty of commercials interrupting your favorite TV shows, but you probably don't realize how many other ads you see. Advertising is everywhere, on posters, in our mail, on the Internet, even on the sides of busses.

Advertising abounds on this busy street corner.

But how does advertising influence us? For one thing, ads make certain products very familiar by showing them to us again and again. For example, there are many brands of soda on the shelves, but if you ask people to name the first two brands that come to mind, 90 percent of them will say Coke and Pepsi, in either order. Why? Because those two companies have spent the most money putting their products in front of us for many years.

Advertisers also influence how we think by giving us reasons to buy their products. For example, an ad's message may be that if you buy a certain product you will look better, smell better, be more fashionable, be more popular, have less to worry about, or have more fun. This may or may not be true, but if the ad makes you think that the product will be good for you in some way, then it has influenced you.

Sometimes advertising can influence us in positive ways. You might learn about new foods that are healthy or about new timesaving technology. You could discover a great place to go on vacation or be influenced to give money to the Red Cross.

Advertising also influences people in negative ways. Beer commercials have led many teens to think it's okay to start drinking alcohol, which is both illegal and dangerous. Advertising also influences people to buy things that they don't really need and cannot afford.

Companies need to advertise to let us know about their products and services. However, we need to make smart decisions and not be influenced too easily by the commercials and print ads we see every day. ■

How Much Is Enough?

Do you think your allowance is a fair amount? Do you have chores you have to do get an allowance? What do you do with your money? These are the kinds of questions we ask about money for our entire lives!

Say you're eight and your mom gives you a dollar every Saturday morning. You don't have to do anything special for it (although it helps not to do any-thing bad during the week). How much will you have after an entire year of Saturdays? Fifty-two dollars! That is if you don't spend any of it along the way.

But when you turn ten, is a dollar a week still fair? Maybe. What if you agreed to clean your room every Saturday morning? That's probably something you should do regularly anyway, but maybe that would convince your mom to double your allowance. That would be two dollars every week! You can figure out how much that would be after a year (remem-ber, no spending).

But maybe you would like to get an even bigger allowance. Now you begin the process that business people call negotiating.

You suggest to your mom that you not only clean your room but also take out the trash every Tuesday morning for a five-dollar-a-week allowance.

Your mom doesn't think that's enough chores for five dollars. So she offers to give you five dollars every Saturday if you clean your room once a week, take the trash out on Tuesdays, and mow the lawn on Thursdays after school. But you hate to mow! So you offer to wash the car instead of mowing. It's a deal!

And if you save all your money in the bank, the bank will pay you money (called interest) to use your money—and you don't have to do a thing! By saving and investing, you can earn money while you lie on your bed and listen to music! ■

The Money Game

The Stock Market is like a grocery store, only the store's products are companies not vegetables. And you don't get to pick up your goods and take them home. You just pick up a small fraction of your product, like one grain of rice grain out of a whole bag. That's because when you buy a stock, you buy only a piece of something much larger—a whole company.

You buy and sell stocks in companies using a stock broker, either a person or a website. Selling stock for more than you bought it for is the secret to making money with the stock market. It also means that buying and selling stock is a risky business.

What Is a Stock?

A company that sells stock is known as a "publicly owned" company. Each stockholder owns a tiny portion of the company—one or more "shares," which is another term for stock. So if you really like a particular company that is publicly owned, you can buy a share (as long as you are 18 years old). Or ten shares. Or a thousand shares, depending on how much money you have.

How Much Is It Worth?

A company's stock is worth what you and everyone else in the world are willing to pay for an ownership share in the company. This is partly determined by how much profit the company makes. A company shows a profit when sales are greater than costs of running the business, leaving some money left over—the profits. Stock prices go up when buyers think a company is making good profits and they are eager to buy a piece of it.

© Corbis

So What Is the Stock Market?

The Stock Market is like a game in which many people are buying and selling stock at the same time. The places where stocks are traded are called exchanges, like The New York Stock Exchange. Each day the newspapers report how much each stock went up or down on different stock exchanges. A few points or a small percentage can make a big difference if you own a lot of shares in a certain company.

Where to Invest

The largest 100 publicly traded companies have been around for many years and many have been good investments, meaning their stock prices have risen. But stocks carry risks: it's not like putting your money in the bank. The value of a stock changes all the time, and prices can go down when business is poor and you can lose your money! ■

Alien Cover-Up?

A rancher heard a loud crash. The air force came to investigate. And people accused the government of hiding the facts about the crash that put Roswell, New Mexico, on the UFO map.

Ever since that night of July 2, 1947, Roswell has been associated with aliens. And the town seems okay with that. It is crawling with UFO stuff. There is the International UFO Museum and Research Center. Every July, Roswell hosts the annual UFO Festival, which includes choosing the Miss UFO Festival beauty queen. You can eat at the Crashdown Café, where a fake UFO is sticking out of the side of the building.

The United States Air Force was said to have first announced that their men had found debris from an alien spacecraft at the crash site. Then the story changed—it was not a spaceship but simply a high-altitude weather balloon gone astray.

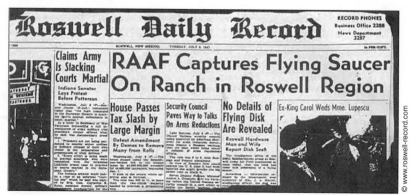
Headline for July 2, 1947

People also believed that the government had captured aliens and was holding them in captivity. Government officials denied that claim. Any potential "aliens," they explained, were probably parachute test dummies.

People who were there the night of the crash said that the government bribed them to hush up about what they knew. The official position of the U.S. Air Force is that there never was any cover-up.

But on the morning of July 8, 1947, The Roswell Daily Record headline said, "Air Force Captures Flying Saucer on Ranch in Roswell Region." And things have never been the same in Roswell. ■

Seeing Aliens

Late on a September night in 1961, Betty and Barney Hill were returning to their home in southern New Hampshire after a short vacation in Canada. The stars were plentiful in the dark sky of the White Mountains. But one was brighter than the rest. And closer. And it was following them! Was it an unidentified flying object, a UFO?

The next thing the Hills knew they were passing through a town thirty miles farther south than they were last conscious of being. And the time was two hours later. What had happened during those two hours they would eventually reveal under hypnosis. Some people believed them. Some didn't. Do you?

The Hills said that after seeing the bright light, they came upon nine "beings" standing in the road. They described them as "bald-headed alien beings, about five foot tall, with grayish skin, pear-shaped heads, and slanting catlike eyes." The aliens took the Hills into their spaceship!

The Hills later explained, each in separate interviews, that inside the spaceship the aliens did simple medical experiments on them. Betty and Barney both described them as friendly and nonthreatening. The aliens showed Betty a "star map," which she recreated while under hypnosis.

Betty and Barney Hill

At first Barney didn't want to tell anyone about their experience, but the next day Betty insisted on calling the local air force base to report the sighting. They then pretended it never happened. Almost two years later, when they had had enough of the inaccurate reporting they were reading in the papers and hearing on the news, Betty and Barney began to speak out about their experience with the UFO. A movie about it called *The UFO Incident* became popular and brought them even more attention.

The Hills' lives were never the same. They began to do lectures about UFOs. They claimed that over the years a bright light often followed them, but the aliens never made contact with them again. After Barney died in 1969, Betty began doing hundreds of lectures a year. Betty died in 2004, at the age of eighty-five. ∎

Magic Women

Although women have been involved with magic since practically the beginning of time, it was usually as an assistant to a male magician. In the 1800s, Adelaide Hermann, who had been her magician husband's assistant, became a headliner when he died and she took over his show. Right now there are an estimated fifty full-time women magicians in the whole world. But few women have become household names like Houdini, David Copperfield, and Siegfried & Roy.

Contemporary female magicians are breaking that mold. Trixie Bond is one of the most successful magicians working today. Every year, she does hundreds of shows for children's birthday parties. Based in Houston, Texas, Trixie has also been a magic consultant for several Hollywood movies.

Jade is a Chinese American woman who has won some of magic's top awards. In 1990, she was the first woman to receive the International Brotherhood of Magicians' World Competition, securing her place in magic history. Jade travels around the world performing at corporate parties and even for royalty.

Magician Dorothy Dietrich's claims to fame include being the first female magician to saw someone in half and to catch a bullet in her teeth. She has done amazing feats like escaping from a straitjacket while hanging upside down from a burning rope. Houdini would be proud!

The role of women in magic may historically have been only as assistants, but they are making their place in magic history now. ■

Trixie Bond in costume

A Master Magician

A straitjacket is a tough canvas coat with extra long sleeves that are attached at the back so the person wearing it cannot move his or her arms. It is very hard to get out of a straitjacket on your own. Harry Houdini amazed the world when he not only did that but did it while hanging upside down by his ankles several feet above the ground! This kind of trick made Houdini the most famous magician ever.

His real specialty was escaping from locked handcuffs. But simply getting out of the handcuffs wasn't enough for Harry. He had to add little twists, like unlocking handcuffs while submerged in a crate sealed with a padlock that he then also had to escape from. That's a hard day's work!

Harry Houdini was born in Hungary, in 1874 (his real name was Erich Weiss) and moved to Wisconsin when he was four years old. He was a small man with a high-pitched voice and little education. He became captivated by magic in the usual way—as a young boy, he saw a magician perform.

Harry was an athletic young man, and he directed his athleticism toward becoming a magician. His magic show was kind of a flop at first. After five years he almost gave it up. But the Needle Trick changed all that. In this magic trick he "swallowed" needles and thread and coughed them back up with all the needles threaded through their eyes! Harry was on his way up.

Houdini at work

© www.houdiniTribute.com

Always making up new, even more amazing stunts kept Harry on magic's cutting edge. In 1907, he jumped handcuffed into San Francisco Bay with a seventy-five-pound ball and chain strapped to his ankles! He lived through that, and in 1910 he escaped out of the mouth of a cannon just before the fuse burned down.

No wonder Harry Houdini became a household name and Houdini is now synonymous with magic. Alas, he died of a ruptured appendix on Halloween day in 1926. ■

A Beloved Loser

A racehorse named Glorious Spring has captivated the entire nation of Japan. Not because she wins racetrack bettors a lot of money. Just the opposite. Glorious Spring has not won a single race in over six years of racing. Her Japanese fans go wild every time she loses.

In her native Japan, Glorious Spring has had a movie made about her. She inspired a popular song. Her image shows up on t-shirts, mugs, you name it. Bettors bet on her just to get a ticket with her name on it. Then they also bet on the horse they really think might win and slip the Glorious Spring ticket in their pocket as a good luck charm. Even Japan's prime minister got "Glorious Spring fever."

Why is a plain chestnut horse who has lost over a hundred times in a row so special to the people of Japan? Some say that as Japan struggles to recover from a bad economy with few jobs and many companies going out of business, Glorious Spring represents the lesson of never giving up.

Glorious Spring usually crosses the finish line in the middle of the pack. Maybe the lesson is that it's okay to be in the middle. That winning isn't everything. And that sometimes not winning is even better!

Whatever the lesson, Glorious Spring doesn't care one way or another. She is beloved by all. She was presented with a huge supply of carrots for being a tourism ambassador. And her owners describe her as "the happiest horse on earth." ∎

Horse Behavior

Kneel on the floor and put your head down as if you are going to pick up small pieces of food with your lips (don't actually do it—eew!). All you can see in this position is the floor. If you really strain your eyes, you can see a few inches around you. That's because we have binocular vision and our eyes are close together on the front of our heads—the best place for them given our upright position.

Horses are perfectly suited for having their heads down—which they do a lot when they are grazing in a pasture. They have an eye on each side of their head; with their head down, horses can see almost completely around them! They have monocular vision—each eye sees individually. Horses see one view of the world from their right side and a different view from their left. They have a small range of binocular vision in front and behind them. Directly in front and directly behind, they can't see a thing—these are called *blind spots.*

To be able to ride a horse safely, it's best to know these things about their vision. When horses are afraid of something, their first instinct is to run away from it. If you are riding a horse and he seems concerned about something in the distance, it can help to turn him in the direction of the thing bothering him so he can focus on the object using his limited binocular vision.

Another important thing to understand about a horse's monocular vision is how it affects his view of what's going on behind him. He may be looking out of his left eye and see, say, a rider in the saddle. Then he turns to the right and Whoa! It's there too! This is often referred to as switching eyes. For the safety of the rider in the saddle, it is important that a young horse first being ridden become comfortable switching eyes. If not, the rider may experience a little unexpected and probably unwanted rodeo action! ■

A Pet Iguana?

So you think you wanna iguana? You might want to think again!

The cute eight-inch reptile at the pet store will grow to an adult size of up to six feet. That means an "ig" needs a pretty big cage; some pet iguanas get their own room in the house! And that room needs to be kept between 70 and 95 degrees at all times.

They also require humidity. Keep the plant mister handy, because you will need to mist your iguana several times a day.

Adult iguanas have sharklike teeth that can bite off a human finger! You will need to train your young ig to be tame and friendly.

And when you're not misting or playing with or controlling the temperature for your iguana, you might be in the kitchen preparing its food. Iguanas cannot eat meat or meat-based food; it will kill them. So get out the food processor (with adult supervision) and start shredding fruits and vegetables like romaine lettuce, squash, melons, spinach, and seedless grapes.

Your iguana will need a pool to soak in. It will also use this pool as a toilet, so you will need to clean it every day. You will need to let it swim in the bathtub regularly. And finally, after a day of controlling the temperature, taming your

Pet iguanas require very special attention.

iguana, misting it, preparing its meals, and changing its wading pool, you'll need to cover its cage—an iguana needs darkness to be able to sleep. That's a lot of care!

Do you still think you wanna iguana? ∎

The Popularity of Pets

If all the people in America who have a dog or a cat raised their hand, there would be around seventy-six million hands in the air! And that's just dogs and cats. Guinea pigs, hamsters, gerbils, sugar gliders, ferrets, and all sorts of reptiles are kept as house pets as well.

Even though we love our pets, millions of them still end up in animal shelters all around the country. Sadly, millions are humanely put to sleep in these shelters because there are just too many unwanted dogs and cats.

What is the first important thing pet owners can do to help reduce the number of animals in the shelters? Spay female and neuter male cats and dogs so that they can't accidentally have kittens and puppies. Leave that to people who have learned to be responsible breeders.

Responsible breeders are careful to breed only those animals that have been tested and shown not to have diseases and conditions that can be genetically passed along to their offspring. They also take excellent care of the young animals. They make sure that the kittens and puppies get the right vaccinations and medical attention at the right times to help them grow up strong and healthy. For the person who will eventually own these pets, these things are really important! The animals will have a better chance of not needing lots of expensive veterinary care.

Most of the dogs available through pet shops are bought cheaply from what are known as *puppy mills*—places

© Getty Images 92060

where female dogs are kept pregnant a lot. The puppy mills and the pet stores often seem to care more about making money than about the quality and well-being of the mother and father and the offspring. And they count on the fact that when you are looking at a cute little puppy it's hard to worry about all of that!

So if you are going to get a pet it is best to go to a reputable breeder. Or you can always give a home to a great dog or cat waiting for you at the local animal shelter! ■

Making Honey

What happens if bees in a hive are overcrowded, lack food, or just plain feel insecure? They swarm! That is, a group of bees leaves the hive to create a new hive. Beekeepers work hard to prevent swarming. The more bees in the hive, the more honey the beekeeper will collect.

Honeybees love violets, forget-me-nots, cornflowers, and, surprise, honeysuckle. A field of clover is like heaven on earth for honeybees. They visit these flowers and collect nectar, which they then turn into honey. But how do they do that?

Bees have a regular stomach like ours. They also have a "honey backpack" in which they store the nectar they collect when they make the rounds of their favorite flowers. When her (all worker bees are female) backpack is full, the bee heads back to the hive.

Another worker bee is waiting to suck the honey out of the returning bee's backpack. She sits around

© Getty Images OS50091

and chews on it for a half hour or so before she deposits it into a bunch of holes in the hive known as a honeycomb. Water evaporates from the chewed-up nectar, making it pretty thick. The bee seals off the hole in the honeycomb with a kind of wax to protect the honey. Then she waits for another bee to arrive with more nectar.

The beekeeper harvests a lot of the honey but leaves enough for the bees to live on during seasons when flowers are not in bloom. ∎

The Super Ant

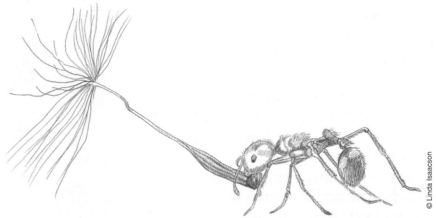

© Linda Isaacson

You have probably seen a single ant scurrying across the kitchen floor. You can be certain that where there is one ant, there are several. Or more like several thousand.

Ants live in colonies. The colony is known as a super-organism. The thousands of ants that make up the colony operate as a unified whole, almost as if they are one organism.

Individual ants sacrifice themselves for the sake of the colony. Each ant has a very specialized job. Some attend to the needs of the colony's queen. She becomes too large to move on her own, so a group of ants may do it for her. Some ants' sole job is to remove eggs as the queen lays them and bring them to a room in the nest called the nursery. Ant attendants in the nursery do nothing else in their entire lives except take care of the colony's larvae.

Other ants have a little more adventure. They spend their lives scouting for food. This adventure comes with peril, however. Like when a giant human shoe comes crashing down on top of them.

Ants are excellent communicators. One of their important methods of communication is touch. An ant's antenna may have as many as thirteen joints, making them superb feelers. Ants spend an incredible amount of time cleaning their antennae, which is a good indication of how important they are.

Ants also communicate by smell. This is how they let other ants know about a good source of food. They don't go back to the nest and explain what the food smells like and where it is. No, the ants who have found the food produce a trail of pheromones, which are like invisible bread crumbs. All the other ants in the colony recognize the scent and follow it to the food.

Smell is so important to ants that if a strange ant walks into a colony of thousands of ants, colony members immediately recognize it as a stranger and drive it out or even kill the intruder. ■

Naming Hurricanes

Agnes. Floyd. Connie. Hugo. These names have gone down in history. Weather history, that is. They are all names of powerful hurricanes.

The names of hurricanes on the Atlantic coast have been chosen by the National Hurricane Center since 1953. Hurricanes used to be given women's names only. Starting in 1979, hurricanes have been named after both men and women.

Hurricane names are rotated every six years. So in 2010, names from 2004 will start around again. That is, unless they have already been used for a storm that hit hard. Then the country affected by the storm can ask the World Meteorological Organization to retire the name for ten years. Just like they retire ballplayers' numbers! Why would they want to do that? Cleanup from these big storms takes a long time. Lawsuits and insurance claims need time to be processed; this way the storm that caused them won't be mixed up with another storm of the same name.

Short names are easier and quicker to write and say when information needs to be passed along

Image courtesy of MODIS Rapid Response Project at NASA/GSFC.

fast. The name Fran was retired in 1996 after Hurricane Fran slammed into North Carolina with deadly force. However, Hurricane Frances showed up on the 2004 hurricane list in the Atlantic. When weather professionals talked about Frances, they shortened it to Fran. That hurricane also turned out to be a big one, so now two powerful Atlantic coast hurricanes known as Fran are in the history books! ■

Hurricane Hunters

Imagine being on a roller coaster. First you go way, way, way up. Then you fly straight down. Now imagine doing that without tracks to guide the roller-coaster car. That's what can happen when you fly an airplane into a hurricane. Who would do such a crazy thing? Hurricane Hunters!

Hurricanes are violent storms with high winds, heavy rain, and sometimes hail. To prepare for a hurricane, people board up the windows in their houses. They bring inside everything that is loose. And then they head for a strong shelter.

But when hurricanes form, pilots from NOAA (the National Oceanographic and Atmospheric Association) and the Air Force head for their airplanes, nicknamed Hurricane Hunters. Their job is to fly right into the hurricanes.

The purpose of these missions is to radio data back to NOAA to be analyzed so the people there can learn how to predict hurricanes better. The information gathered from hurricane flights has already helped the National Weather Service be able to warn people further in advance of a coming hurricane and tell them how strong it is, its intensity. This information helps save people's property and their lives.

The high winds and heavy rain of a hurricane swirl around from right to left, or counterclockwise, creating a calm

A typical NOAA "Hurricane Hunter" airplane

Hurricane Research Division, Atlantic Oceanographic and Meteorological Laboratory, NOAA, U.S. Department of Commerce.

spot in the very center called the eye of the storm. The Hurricane Hunters fly into the hurricane, through turbulent air in what is called the eye wall, and then into the eye. The roller-coaster part comes when air pockets create downdrafts and updrafts, sometimes causing the plane to lurch hundreds of feet!

Each mission lasts for around ten hours. Even though their job is a pretty daring one, Hurricane Hunter pilots are very cautious. They take lots of safety precautions, and they always plan an escape route out of the hurricane.

Colonel Joseph Duckworth was the first person to fly into a hurricane, in 1943. Even though it sounds like a really dangerous thing to do, only one Hurricane Hunter plane has been lost in an Atlantic Coast hurricane in over sixty years. ■

Real Giants

Imagine a tree as wide as a car is long. And as tall as a twenty-five-story building. That is what you could expect to see if you were looking at one of the giant sequoias, the largest trees in the world.

Giant sequoias are found in the national parks of central and northern California. They average around 250 feet tall and 25 feet around. It would take you and eight or nine of your friends to join hands to wrap your arms around a giant sequoia!

Some of these trees have been alive for more than three thousand years. How do they manage to live so long? For one thing, their thick bark is fire-resistant, allowing them to withstand forest fires. The bark is also resistant to many of the diseases that kill other types of trees. In addition, the government has made it illegal to cut down a giant sequoia.

You won't find a giant sequoia all alone. They grow in groups called groves. A single grove may have as few as ten trees or as many as twenty thousand!

The massive trees were named for Chief Sequoia of the Cherokee Indians. And some of the trees themselves have individual names. Like General Sherman, the largest

Some giant sequoias are large enough to drive through!

of the giant sequoias, at nearly 275 feet tall and 32 feet in diameter. There are also trees named Lincoln, Washington, King Arthur, and General Grant.

If you visit places like Sequoia National Park or Yosemite National Park, you can visit some of these trees yourself! ∎

The Power of Niagara Falls

Every second, 1.5 million gallons of water pour over Niagara Falls, the most powerful waterfalls (there are three in all) in the world. Niagara Falls sit on the border between the United States and Canada. The three falls are the Canadian Falls, also known as the Horseshoe Falls because of their shape; the American Falls; and a smaller waterfall called the Bridal Falls. The Canadian Falls are by far the largest, spanning more than 2,000 feet in length with a drop of 176 feet.

The Niagara Falls are the most powerful waterfalls in the world.

More than twelve million people visit Niagara Falls each year. Most visitors look down at the falls from either Canada or the United States, and many take a tour on a boat that travels through the waters below. A few people, however, have tried to go over the falls.

In 1901, a sixty-three-year old grandmother climbed into a barrel and went over the Horseshoe Falls. She survived the stunt, becoming the first person to make it over the large waterfall. Others have tried since, some of whom were killed by the power of the waterfalls and the rocks below. Those who have survived were promptly arrested, since going over the falls is illegal.

Besides being a spectacular sight, the Niagara Falls are also a major supplier of power. Two hydroelectric plants, one in Canada and one in the United States, use the power of the surging water to generate electricity for millions of people in both countries.

Many people wonder if the waterfalls stop during the icy winters. Only once, in 1848, did ice in the river stop the falls. Typically, ice forms along the banks of the river and slowly stretches from one side to the other to form an ice bridge, but it doesn't stop the falls. Visitors used to walk on the ice bridges for many years, until an ice bridge broke in 1912 and killed three people.

The Niagara Falls remain one of the most spectacular sites in nature, worth visiting by day or night. At night, bright lights illuminate the great falls in many colors. ■

What's Your Type?

Although your blood type is not as unique as your fingerprints, there are four different human blood types: A, B, AB, and O.

In the early 1900s, Karl Landsteiner noticed that different samples of blood contained different molecules. Some had a molecule he called A. Others didn't have A, but had a different molecule, so he called that *B*. Some had both—*AB*. And some had neither—*O!* He won a Nobel Prize for this discovery.

Some blood types are interchangeable. Someone with type A blood can donate blood to a person with either type A or type AB. A person with type B blood can donate to type B or type AB. But a person with type AB can only donate blood to another person with type AB. Type O can donate to all three others but can only receive type O. A person with type AB blood can receive a donation from anyone! Mixing blood types that don't go together is dangerous.

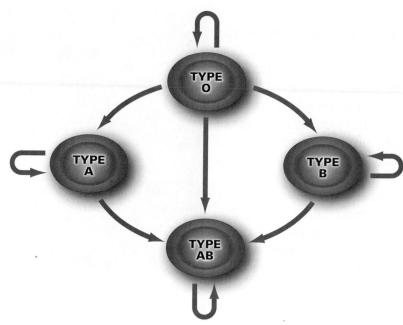

Blood type interaction model

If a person receives the wrong blood type in a process called a transfusion, the person's immune system will attack it with antibodies, making the blood clot when it shouldn't.

But wait, it gets even more complicated. Scientists found a certain kind of protein in the blood they named the Rh factor (after the Rhesus monkeys they studied to discover it). If your blood contains this protein, your blood type will be marked with a + sign, like A+ (A positive). If your blood does not have the Rh protein, it is marked with a negative sign (A-). ■

Your Circulatory System

The circulatory system is a lot like the plumbing in your house. Good clean water comes into the house from either a well or a city water supply. The water circulates through the house in the pipes and valves of the plumbing system, supplying the house's "organs"—your bathtub, sinks, clothes washer, and so on. Dirty water leaves these "organs" and goes through different pipes in the plumbing system out of the house and into the septic tank or city sewer. There the water is cleaned up and eventually makes it back into the ground where it will someday once again be picked up by a plumbing system.

Your blood—a little more than five quarts of it—circulates through your body's organs where its oxygen gets used and it picks up some waste products. The plumbing of your circulatory system leads back to the heart. When the blood arrives in the heart, it makes a quick trip to the lungs through the *pulmonary artery*, where the blood gets fresh oxygen and gets rid of some of the wastes. The cleaned-up blood goes back to a different area of the heart where it gets pumped out again to the rest of the body. And the process happens all over again.

Veins are the blood vessels that bring blood from the rest of the body into the heart. Arteries carry blood away from the heart and out to the body. The human body has thousands of miles of blood vessels!

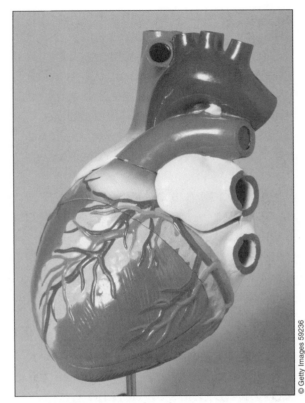

A model of the human heart

We should be thankful that the heart is made up of incredibly strong muscles that work tirelessly all the time, day and night. It beats around three billion times in the average person's lifetime! All the more reason to eat good food, get plenty of exercise, and help your heart stay strong and healthy. ■

Gypsy Musician

Gypsies live a hard, traveling life and rarely become famous. But Django Reinhardt was an exception. Although he couldn't read or write for most of his life, he was an incredible musician. His jazzlike musical style continues to be loved around the world long after his death in 1953.

Django was born in Belgium in a caravan—he didn't live in a real house until he was twenty years old! In 1918, his parents moved to France and joined the Manouche gypsies outside Paris. He got his first musical instrument when he was twelve years old, and it quickly became clear he had talent.

But things weren't going to be easy for Django. When he was eighteen he was badly burned in a caravan fire, leaving his left pinky and ring fingers permanently curled. Django didn't give up music though! He simply developed a unique guitar-playing technique that would become his graceful and creative signature style.

In 1934, Django and another guitarist began a band called the Quintet of the Hot Club of France.

© Getty Images OS34108

Their records were hits! He never heard real American jazz until he was twenty-three, when someone played him a record by Louis Armstrong. He was hooked. Django visited the United States just once after World War II, when he played Carnegie Hall with Duke Ellington.

But it was in France where Django thrived. He became a sensation in his day, and his gypsy music has a new following with every new generation. ■

Music with a Cause

Music has been called a universal language. That may be why music has often been used to help call attention to a social or political situation.

Band Aid was the name given to the group of musicians who got together in 1984 to record a single song to raise money to help starving victims of the famine in Ethiopia, Africa.

This idea led to another one—a fundraising concert called Live Aid. The Live Aid concert took place on July 13, 1985, in London and Philadelphia. It was broadcast via satellite to over one and a half billion listeners and viewers around the world. They raised over 140 million dollars to help the people of Africa.

From the Live Aid idea came Farm Aid. The first concert was on Sept 22, 1985, in Illinois. Bob Dylan, Billy Joel, B. B. King. Willie Nelson, Neil Young, John Mellencamp, and many other famous musicians have kept the idea going to this day. Farm Aid assistance helps farmers through tough times like droughts, floods, and other natural disasters or large drops in crop prices.

Famous entertainer Bill Cosby and a whole bunch of hip-hop musicians have taken on the idea of music for a cause.

Live concerts are often used as fundraisers.

They are eager to promote a positive outlook to young people in cities to help reduce violence and gang participation and increase educational achievement. They created Hip Hop for the P.E.O.P.L.E., which will produce a documentary film and a hip-hop CD.

Aid through music happens on a smaller scale as well. A group of opera singers came together in England in 1994 and created the Fettucine Opera Company. They regularly perform small dinner concerts for donations to charitable causes. ■

The History of Photography

Sit perfectly still and say cheese for eight hours straight. That's what it was like to have your picture taken back in 1827. The photograph came out on a plate, one of a kind, sort of like a painting.

The earliest negative—the film that you can use to duplicate the same picture many times—was developed in 1835. As with most inventions, the quality of the early negatives was not very good. But that changed very quickly.

To operate a camera, you used to have to know about exposure times and the chemicals used in processing film. But a man by the name of George Eastman created cameras that even your kid brother could figure out how to use. He called his company Eastman Kodak.

Advancements in photography haven't slowed down much. Just when we thought one-hour processing and disposable cameras were the cutting edge, along came digital photography. Now you can even buy disposable digital cameras!

Photography allows us to record and remember family events. And it has recorded some incredible moments in history. For example,

The first cameras were much bigger than the ones we use today.

from 1861–65, photographer Matthew Brady exposed seven thousand negatives as he covered the Civil War.

Not everyone thought photography was wonderful. Artists who made money painting portraits were worried that photography would threaten their livelihood. The Bible's prohibition against "graven images" made some people think photography was the work of the devil. But with billions of pictures taken each year, most people must believe it's a good thing! ∎

Flemish Painters: Artistic Survivors

Back in the 1500s, the northern portion of the European country Belgium was known as Flanders. From Flanders came the term *Flemish*. The Flemish painters, often referred to as the Dutch Masters because of their ancestry, had a huge influence on the history of painting.

Going to School

Art periods are often referred to as *schools,* and the Flemish school of painting was a significant one. What does Flemish art look like? Think of realistic landscapes in dark tones and portraits of people with billowing dresses and hats with large feathers sticking out of them. Schools of painting change, and the Flemish school was no exception. In the later years, landscapes were no longer void of people, and people were no longer painted in isolation; figures were integrated into elaborate landscapes.

Brink of Destruction

Flemish art of these early years almost didn't survive. In 1566, during a period of iconoclasm, when religious monuments and icons are being destroyed, much magnificent early Flemish artwork was destroyed. But the Flemish painters seemed to have survived by moving their artistic center to a different city every few hundred years—usually the city in which the current Dutch Master lived.

Changing Masters

From the late fifteenth century to the early sixteenth century, Bruges was the Flemish painters' mecca. One of the most

Rembrandt

famous Flemish painters, Jan van Eyck, had settled there and established the school of Bruges. Considered one of the greatest masters, van Eyck was one of the first artists to use oil paints. In the early 1500s, Antwerp took over as the center of Flemish painting, with the master Quentin Massys.

Perhaps the most famous Dutch painter is Rembrandt. Although Dutch, Rembrandt is considered a Baroque-style painter, a period ushering in the 1600s, following on the heels of the Flemish school. ■

The Tour de France

The bicycle race called the Tour de France is known as the toughest sports event in the world. It started in 1903 and takes place every year, in July.

The Tour de France crosses several of the Alps mountains; 2,290 miles and three weeks later it ends in downtown Paris! Over two hundred riders race, and thousands of people from around the world line the roads, cheering on their favorite racers.

But the race isn't just one long ride to see who gets to Paris first. Each day a new race, called a *stage,* begins. During a mountain stage the riders climb a mountain. For a time-trial stage the riders sprint shorter distances, racing against the clock. During some stages they just cover a certain number of miles. There are a couple of rest days too. Whew!

Each stage has a winner. Some riders are better at climbing, some at sprinting, so the rider who wins a stage may not be the overall leader. Each day, whoever is the overall leader wears a special yellow jersey.

The Tour de France covers 2,290 miles in France.

You may think of bicycle racing as an individual sport. But in a race like the Tour de France, riders are members of a team. Teamwork is critical to winning. Team members help their best rider conserve energy by pulling him along in an air pocket called a *draft.* Or they help protect him from running into something and taking a spill.

Some famous Tour de France winners are Eddie Merckx, Greg LeMond, and Lance Armstrong. ■

Racing for Life

One day you are a professional athlete heading toward the peak of your career; the next you are a cancer patient fighting for your life. That's how it was for professional cyclist Lance Armstrong.

Made for Cycling

From the time he was a young boy, Lance's body seemed made for cycling—not only is he tall and long-legged, but tests show that his lungs take in and use more oxygen than normal. This makes his muscles work more efficiently, so they don't tire and cramp as easily.

After struggling as a young racer Lance gained experience and maturity, and he began to win. A lot. He set a goal to ride in the 1997 Tour de France, a race described as the most grueling sports event in the world. The Tour de France goes through the Alps mountain range in Europe. The race lasts for three weeks and is 2,290 miles long! It ends in downtown Paris.

The End of a Career?

But the year before, while conditioning, Lance began to feel very tired. He finally went to a doctor, and everything changed: Lance was diagnosed with cancer. Everyone assumed his cycling career was over. He thought maybe even his life was over.

Doctors performed delicate surgery to remove tumors on his brain. Chemotherapy treatment, which kills cancer cells but kills a lot of good cells too, made this once strong athlete unable even to crawl out of his hospital bed.

But Lance and his doctors fought hard and beat cancer. Then he slowly returned to bicycle racing. That was

Cyclists ride 2,290 miles in the Tour de France.

© Getty Images 1081

hard too. He quit a couple of times. But he had one good day. And then another. One ride at a time, Lance got hooked on bicycle racing again—and he hadn't forgotten his quest to win that toughest bicycle race in the world, the Tour de France.

A Fantastic Comeback

In 1999, Lance not only competed, he won. He won again in 2000, and again in 2001 and 2002. In 2003, he tied the record of five Tour de France wins. And in 2004, Lance beat the record and won the Tour de France for the sixth straight time.

Lance had won two grueling races—the one in sports and the one for his life. ■

Oscar Schindler

A dark period of world history took place in the mid-1900s, when Adolf Hitler killed millions of Jewish people in concentration camps in Europe. But one man did his best to save people from the gas chambers.

Oscar Schindler was a shrewd businessman. He profited greatly from World War II, eventually opening a cookware factory for making mess kits and other military products. The Jewish workers he hired to make the goods were given their lives in return. Oscar Schindler spared no expense in keeping the people who worked for him safe from harm.

How did Schindler save hundreds of Jews while millions were being transported to Hitler's death camps? Schindler had a reputation for being a partying man who loved extravagance. He joined the Nazi party not because he believed in it but because he thought it would help him get rich. He was well liked by high-ranking

International Memorial in Dachau, Germany

© Nandor Gild/Corbis

Germans, and he used his influence to gain favors. Schindler bribed Nazi officials. And he lied—his factory did make things needed for the war effort but it employed more workers than necessary.

Eventually, Oscar Schindler created a list of all the people who worked for him in his factory. He circulated this list to Nazi officials, who made sure the people on it weren't sent to the gas chambers. The list became known as Schindler's List.

Oscar Schindler died in 1974, penniless, but a hero in the eyes of the world. ■

The Importance of Hard Work

Wilma Rudolph was diagnosed with polio at the age of five. Doctors said she would never walk. But her mother, her 21 siblings, and her own discipline and willpower changed all that.

After years of therapy and wearing a metal brace, at age 12 Wilma decided to take the brace off and try walking without it. Not only could she walk, but she began to play basketball also! A coach from Tennessee State University invited her to run on the college's track team before she had graduated high school.

Wilma was so fast she qualified for the 1956 Olympics, where she won a bronze medal in the 400-meter relay. In 1960, Wilma qualified for the Olympics again. She became the first woman to ever win three gold medals at an Olympics. The next time that feat was accomplished was in 1988, by runner Jackie Joyner-Kersee.

Wilma went from struggling to walk with a leg brace to being known as "the fastest woman in the world." She won many sports awards, including the Associated

Wilma Rudolph at the finish line during 50 yard dash at track meet in Madison Square Garden

Press Woman Athlete of the Year award in 1960. She was inducted into the National Women's Hall of Fame in 1994, the same year she died of brain cancer.

Her sports achievements were great but Wilma's life was filled with many accomplishments. Upon returning home from the Rome Olympics in 1960, she refused to attend her hometown celebration if it was segregated; so that event became the first integrated event ever in Clarksville, Tennessee. And Wilma established the Wilma Rudolph Foundation, whose purpose was to help children learn the importance of hard work and discipline. ■

On the Wings of a Dream

Could you imagine being the first person ever to fly an airplane? Not only did Wilbur and Orville Wright imagine flying, they made those dreams come true. From the time they were young boys and their father bought them a toy that could fly across the living room, they were convinced that they would create a machine in which man could fly.

The idea of flying posed a great challenge to inventors, scientists, and daredevils from all over the world. Many of them had tried unsuccessfully to find a way to fly throughout the nineteenth century. So when the Wright brothers started out in 1899 on their quest to invent the airplane, they began by studying why all of the previous attempts failed. They also learned about the first hot-air balloons and about the gliders that had flown successfully powered by the wind. They even studied kites.

Finally, in 1903, they developed a motorized aircraft with a propeller that they knew would fly. On December 17, 1903, the Wright brothers made four brief but historic flights at Kitty Hawk, North Carolina, with their first powered aircraft, called the Wright Flyer. They had invented the first airplane.

Orville and Wilbur knew that they would need to improve upon these short straight flights at Kitty Hawk if they wanted to sell their invention to companies that would build airplanes. So they went back to work on their invention.

The Wright Flyer

In 1905 Wilbur made a spectacular flight in the new version of the Wright Flyer. This time he circled the field thirty times and flew nearly twenty-five miles in the process. This was indeed the airplane that they had wanted to invent.

Although the early flights of the Wright brothers did not get a lot of immediate attention, the brothers would go on to patent their invention and show people in Europe and throughout the United States that the airplane was a reality.

In 2003 there were centennial celebrations commemorating one hundred years of flight since the Wright Flyer took off and flew, in 1903. ■

The Life of Frida Kahlo

Bright colors and shocking subjects are trademarks of the artwork of Mexican painter Frida Kahlo. Her art seems to reflect the drama of her life. Frida developed polio when she was six years old, which left her with one leg much thinner than the other. When she was eighteen, she was in a serious bus accident; she was bedridden for many months, and her injuries caused her tremendous pain and fatigue throughout the rest of her life.

An Artistic Recovery

While Frida lay in bed recovering from the accident, she started painting. A friend convinced her to show her paintings to the famous Mexican artist Diego Rivera. They fell in love and were married in 1929, when Frida was nineteen years old. Or maybe she was twenty-two. No one knows for sure, since she lied about her birth date!

Artists in Love

Until she married Diego, Frida kept her black hair cropped short and dressed in men's-style clothing. But Diego convinced her to let her hair grow long and to wear the traditional brightly colored dresses favored by Mexican women.

Frida and Diego were each other's greatest artistic admirers. However, their marriage was a stormy one. They lived a wild life. They were even accused of murdering the communist leader Leon Trotsky, who stayed with them whenever he visited Mexico. Frida's art became world famous; when she visited Europe, she was entertained by contemporaries like Pablo Picasso.

Portrait of Diego Rivera and Frida Rivera

First Exhibit

In 1953, Frida had her first and only exhibition of her paintings in Mexico City. She was very sick, and her doctor ordered her to stay in bed. So Frida arranged an ambulance to bring her to the opening of her exhibit. They set her stretcher up in the middle of the room; from there Frida partied and entertained people with stories until late into the night.

Young Death

Frida died when she was forty-seven. She remained flamboyant even then. As mourners stood by the cremation incinerator, a huge blast of heat made her body rise bolt upright. Her long, black hair was engulfed in flames around her head. At least that's how the story goes! ■

September 11, 2001

September 11, 2001, dawned a picture-perfect late summer Tuesday morning across the United States. But the day quickly unfolded into a tragedy felt around the world. In just over an hour an incredible chain of events took place.

Timeline of Terror

8:45 a.m.: American Airlines Flight 11 crashed straight into the upper floors of the north tower of the World Trade Center, in New York City.

9:03 a.m.: United Airlines Flight 175 crashed into the south tower of the World Trade Center, in New York City.

9:17 a.m.: The Federal Aviation Administration shut down all New York City airports and closed all NYC tunnels and bridges.

9:40 a.m.: All airspace in the United States was shut down, for the first time ever.

9:43 a.m.: American Flight 77 crashed into the Pentagon, in Washington D.C.

9:45 a.m.: The White House was evacuated.

10:10 a.m.: United Flight 93 crashed in a field in Pennsylvania, presumably having been headed for another Washington target.

Tragic Results

No one survived the airplane crashes. Thousands of additional people died, trapped in the burning World Trade Center towers, and caught in the area of the Pentagon where the airplane hit.

Little pieces of the giant puzzle began to be revealed. By day's end, almost all of the nineteen airplane hijackers had been identified, caught on tape passing through security checkpoints and boarding planes.

© Getty Images 5145

Surprise Statement

One more element in the timeline started an ongoing controversy: at 4:20 that afternoon, Senator Bob Graham, of Florida, stated that he wasn't surprised there was an attack by the radical group al-Qaida. Bob Graham had been chair of the U.S. Senate Intelligence Committee, which had warned that al-Qaida leader Osama bin Laden was formulating a plan to hijack U.S. airplanes and use them to attack us, although no specifics like date and location were known.

Prevention?

Could September 11 have been prevented? Theories will circulate forever, and we will probably never know for sure. But one interruption in the chain of events—for example, if one of the hijackers had been detained by security and not allowed to board the airplane—and the day may have been just another beautiful Tuesday. ■

How Computers Work

Computers are everywhere—in classrooms, offices, homes, even cars. From solving difficult scientific equations to playing games, there are thousands of uses for computers. But do you know how a computer works?

Computers take in information, called *data*, through input devices. The most common input devices are the keyboard and the mouse. However, you can also input data through joysticks, bar code readers (used in stores), digital cameras, CDs, scanners, and software programs.

Good Memory

Once you input data into the computer it is stored in one of the computer's memory systems. ROM, read-only memory, is permanent memory that cannot be erased or changed. This controls the start-up process of the computer and other permanent functions like input and output.

RAM, random-access memory, is the memory that controls the current activities of the computer. The operating system—Windows, for example—is controlled by RAM and so are the many different programs you use.

Brain Power

But how does the information know where to go or which memory to use? The answer is simple. The computer has a brain. Okay, it's not a real brain, but it's a microchip known as the CPU, or *central processing unit*. This is the most important part of a computer, because it reads all the computer functions (in computer language) and determines what functions to perform and where the data goes. If, for example, the program has mathematical formulas, the CPU will

© Getty Images 107052

read them and calculate the formulas. Whatever is necessary, the CPU will determine what to do.

Using the Information

In the end, the data comes back from the computer through an output device. The most common output device is your computer screen, or monitor. However, your printer and speakers are also output devices. You can also send the computer output data onto a CD or a disk to be stored for future use.

Of course, all this computer activity, from inputting data to the CPU's reading the computer language and determining what to do with the data to memory storage and outputting the data back to you, typically takes a mere fraction of a second. ■

The Greenhouse Effect

If you've ever been inside of a greenhouse, your first words were probably, "Wow, it's hot in here!" A greenhouse is built of glass and it heats up because lots of sunlight gets in, warming the ground and plants inside. However, the warm air has no way to escape. It's similar to a car that's been parked in the sun for hours with the windows closed—the temperature rises because the heat has no way to get out.

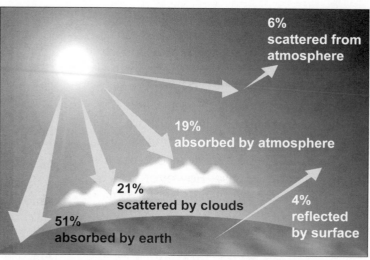

Light from the sun heats up the Earth and surrounding atmosphere.

Help from the Atmosphere

The planet Earth is surrounded by our atmosphere, which traps heat in a way similar to a greenhouse. The sun radiates energy, in the form of light, that passes right through our atmosphere and heats up the Earth's surface. Much of the sun's energy is absorbed by land, oceans, trees, and other plants. The earth also radiates some energy back into space, but in the form of heat instead of light. The atmosphere absorbs some of this heat and warms up. If it weren't for our atmosphere, the Earth would be almost 50 degrees Fahrenheit colder than it is now. This warming is called the *Greenhouse Effect,* and we couldn't live on the Earth without it.

The Role of Gases

The atmosphere is made up of a mixture of different gases; it's about three quarters nitrogen and one quarter oxygen. Oxygen and nitrogen, however, aren't very good at absorbing heat. Most of the heat absorbed by the atmosphere is collected by small amounts of other gases such as methane, nitrous oxide, and above all, carbon dioxide. These gases are unusual in that they are transparent to solar energy, but absorb heat energy. Therefore, they don't block out light from the sun, but they catch the heat as it's radiated back by the earth and keep it in the atmosphere. They are called *greenhouse gases.*

Outside Influences

Carbon dioxide and other greenhouse gases are a natural part of our atmosphere, but they can also be produced by factories, cars, and coal-burning power plants. Over the past century humans have been creating more and more greenhouse gases as the number of cars and factories increases, and many scientists are worried that these man made gases may absorb even more heat and warm the Earth to record levels. This is called the *Enhanced Greenhouse Effect* and its result is what's known as "global warming."

Adapting to global warming will be difficult, and many people are working to find ways to cut back on the amount of greenhouse gases that we are putting into our atmosphere. ■

Ozone Hole

A Hole Lot of Problems

There's a hole in the atmosphere and human beings put it there. We can keep it from getting worse by changing the way we do certain things.

Where is the ozone and its hole? And why do we care?

The Earth's Atmosphere

The atmosphere around the earth is divided into several layers. The closest layer is the first six miles of atmosphere called the *troposphere,* where we live.

Next is the *stratosphere.* This atmospheric layer stretches from 6 to 31 miles above Earth and is where the supersonic jet, the Concorde, cruised.

The Ozone Hole

Ozone molecules are three oxygen atoms stuck together. A little bit of ozone floats around in the troposphere, where we refer to it as smog. But 90% of all ozone is floating in the stratosphere, where it clumps together in different thicknesses in different seasons. And at some times of the year in the last couple of decades, the ozone layer over the Antarctic and the Arctic has been thinner than it has been in the past. The thinning of the ozone is the "hole." And the hole is caused by certain products and how we use them.

How the Hole Got There

The principle cause of the ozone hole is synthetic chemicals, especially chlorine-containing chemicals called ChloroFluoroCarbons (or CFCs.) These chemicals destroy ozone. CFCs had many characteristics that led them to be used in dozens of applications, such as refrigeration and air conditioning, which then led to an explosion in their production. They also used to be found in

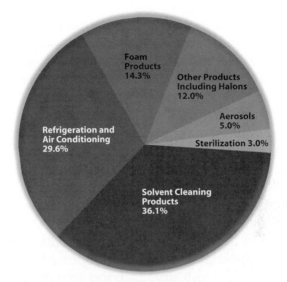

Sources that Harm the Protective Ozone Layer (Data from The Ozone Hole Inc.)

dozens of different aerosols that we use every day in our homes.

A study of the effects of CFCs released into the stratosphere led to a proposed gradual ban of the substances in the so-called Copenhagen Agreement, which would eliminate the use of CFCs by 2030.

Why Do We Care?

What is it about the ozone that makes us so concerned about protecting it? It protects us. The ozone layer is sort of like a giant layer of sunscreen over the earth, blocking harmful ultraviolet rays from the sun from reaching us. Depleting the ozone layer will allow UV rays to reach earth. Our bodies are not designed to withstand the effects of UV light. Without this ozone protection, we would see an increase in things like skin cancer and eye damage. ∎

The Textile Industry

People have been weaving natural fibers into fabric—called textiles—almost since the beginning of human existence. The Chinese produced silk using a silk-reeling machine as early at the first century B.C.

Waterpower became a common power source between the fifth and sixth centuries. The first textile factories in Europe appeared in Italy in the 13th century, which came to be called the Medieval Industrial Revolution.

In the 15th century, wool production emerged as a critical development in the textile industry. England was the first major wool producer but the industry soon spread to other parts of Europe.

As the standard of living rose, demand for textiles grew once again and fueled significant inventions. In 1733, John Kay invented the flying shuttle, which doubled production by allowing one weaver to do the work that formerly took two people. The flying shuttle also doubled the width of the cloth, which formerly was limited to the width of the weaver's outstretched arms.

By the mid-1800s, Britain became major producers of cotton fabric. Most of the raw material for the huge British cotton industry came from the United States. But the Civil War in the 1860s brought that to an end—the North had its own industrial revolution fueled largely by a substantial textile industry. They wanted the cotton for their own mills and prevented the South from exporting the raw cotton grown there.

By the 19th century, the U.S. was becoming the leader in inventing textile-making machinery. Lowell, Massachusetts

Garment worker finishing coats

was incorporated in 1826 as the first planned industrial city in the U.S. The express purpose for the creation of the city of Lowell was to manufacture cloth.

In order for the huge mill complexes to have the workers they needed, women were hired in large numbers . Young women left their homes and flocked to Lowell and surrounding towns in Massachusetts, as well as Manchester, New Hampshire, to work in the mills. Many of these young women were orphans or were fleeing abusive homes. Those struggling with poverty often came to work in the mills in order to relieve the family of a mouth to feed and to send money home. During this time period, it was not considered necessary to educate girls and some went to work in the mills to put their brothers through college.

Even though the girls were allowed and even encouraged to go to evening concerts and events, the workday was long. They were awakened by 4:30 a.m. and expected to be at their machines the mills by 5:30. The mills shut down the machines at 7 p.m.; the girls had from 7 to 10 p.m. and Sundays to themselves.

Even very young girls worked in the mills. Ten-year-olds often served as "bobbin girls." The bobbin girls' work consisted of removing full bobbins of yarn from the spinning machines and replacing them with empty ones. The bobbin girls worked around 15 minutes out of every hour. During the second half of the 19th century, immigrants from Ireland, Scotland, Germany, Sweden, and Canada started to replace the mill girls.

Another significant event in textile mill history happened in 1957—the only anthrax epidemic ever recorded in the United States. Anthrax is a disease that can be carried in sheep's wool. Even though a vaccine was in the process of being tested, five people in the Arms Textile Mill in Manchester, New Hampshire, contracted a form

of anthrax called "inhalation anthrax." None of the five people were part of the vaccination test since they were newly immigrated. Four of them died. The mill was eventually burned to the ground because people still worried that anthrax lurked there, even though it had been thoroughly disinfected.

Textiles continue to be a significant worldwide industry even today. In the 1960s, the World Trade Organization created a global agreement limiting the amount of textiles that could be imported and exported. The agreement was intended to protect countries that rely on a textile industry from being forced out of business by cheaper imports. That agreement came to an end on January 1, 2005.

From jeans to car seats to sofas, rugs, and curtains, textiles are everywhere. The textile industry was largely responsible for the rapid increase in new technology and the birth of the Industrial Revolution. And there does not seem to be any foreseeable risk of an invention that will bring the textile industry to an end. ■